Twisted Wisdom
Modern Anti-Proverbs

Wolfgang Mieder
Anna Tóthné Litovkina

Twisted Wisdom
Modern Anti-Proverbs

DeProverbio.com

2002

De Proverbio.com

Hobart, Tasmania (Australia)

DeProverbio.com is an imprint of *De Proverbio* (www.deproverbio.com)

ISBN 1-875943-43-9

First published 1999 by "Proverbium" in corporation with the International Studies
Program, The University of Vermont, Burlington, Vermont, USA

The cover illustration is a reproduction of a German postcard from around 1993.

Introduction

Proverbs have never been considered as absolute truths by the people. While people have appreciated the didactic wisdom of these sapiential gems, they have certainly also noticed the limited scope of proverbs when interpreted as universal laws of behavior. The folk does not consider proverbs sacrosanct, and people are well aware of the fact that proverbs at times are simply too rigid and limited in their prescribed wisdom. Anybody can quickly tell that many proverbs contradict each other, as can be seen by the juxtaposition of such frequently cited proverb pairs as "Out of sight, out of mind" and "Absence makes the heart grow fonder;" "Look before you leap" and "He who hesitates is lost;" and "Barking dogs don't bite" and "A dog will bark before it bites." But such proverbial dueling with opposite or contradictory proverbs is only one of the many ways in which people have reacted humorously or satirically to this storehouse of folk wisdom.

There also exists a long tradition of parodies of individual proverbs by adding contradictory comments to them. In fact, some of these humorous statements have in the meantime become proverbial in themselves, as for example "Absence makes the heart grow fonder - for somebody else," "Every dog has his day, and the cats their nights," and "Love is blind, but neighbors aren't." Just as widespread is the parodistic tradition of reacting to proverbs by changing their interior in one way or another. Very popular are variations that keep the first part of the proverb while replacing the second half, as for example "Early to bed and early to rise and you never meet any prominent people," "If at first you don't succeed, you're average," and "To err is human, but to really screw things up you need a computer." Completing half-stated proverbs has become a party game of sorts, and teachers have also used this method to see whether children still know proverbs or simply to encourage their imaginative thoughts. Some of the resulting texts are most charming and telling: "A rolling stone plays a guitar," "A bird in the hand is warm" and "Man does not live by getting married." Naturally such variations are usually individual occurrences, and only very few, if any, will ever become proverbial in their own right. What all such playful or serious proverb alterations show is that modern people are very much aware of traditional proverbs, so much so in fact, that they enjoy such intentional changes to create innovative communicative devices.

Perhaps a bit more sophisticated are proverb parodies which pervert the basic meaning of a given text by merely changing one word, as in "Where there's a will, there's a won't," "A condom a day keeps the doctor away" and "Necessity is the mother of tension." And even more intriguing are such masterful puns with proverbs in which only one letter of the alphabet needs to be changed in order to render a strikingly new message: "Better mate than never," "Clarity begins at home" and "Expedience is the best teacher." Yet the majority of the twisted proverbs assembled in this collection simply follow the structure of citing the proverbs in their original wording and then adding a statement which puts its wisdom into question or negates it completely. Often such short commentaries are introduced by the conjunction "but," thus immediately flagging the contradictory intent of the message: "Money talks, but it doesn't always talk sense," "Actions speak louder than words, but not nearly as often" and "A new broom sweeps clean, but an old broom knows all the corners." Conjunctions like "and," "if," and "(al)though" are also employed, and at times a mere colon or hyphen are used to connect the rejoinder to the well-known proverb.

Mention should also be made of the fact that we have included in this book a few jokes based on proverbs as well as some so-called wellerisms. The latter are traditional triadic structures which often start with a proverb, followed by a speaker, and then by a situation which places the proverb in a humorous or contradictory situation, as for example in "'Everyone to his taste', said the farmer and kissed the cow" or "'One good turn deserves another', as the alderman said when he discharged the thief who voted for him." While there exists a folk tradition of such wellerisms, people continue to invent statements based on this structural pattern to parody traditional wisdom.

Many of these humorous proverb parodies are based on mere puns and wordplay, but there are also numerous satirical "anti-proverbs," as we like to call them, that contain revealing social comments. In that respect even the anti-proverbs, by which we mean any intentional proverb variation in the form of puns, alterations, deletions or additions, can become moralistic if not didactic statements. Such innovative texts as "Count your pennies and the taxes will take care of themselves," "A woman's place is in the House ... and in the Senate" and "Better safe sex than sorry" contain new wisdom based on traditional proverbial structures. These patterns are used as ready-made formulas to express human thoughts and feelings on a wide spectrum, from philosophical thought to obscenity. Just as well-known proverbs continue to comment about our daily life, so do new anti-proverbs by using alienating and shocking linguistic strategies.

The hundreds of texts assembled in this collection of anti-proverbs represent the first such compilation in the English language. While Wolfgang Mieder has published several collections of German anti-proverbs in Germany since 1982, and while proverb scholars have accepted his term of anti-proverbs as a general description of such innovative alterations of and reactions to traditional proverbs, nobody has hitherto put together a collection of the rich Anglo-American materials. This book then is merely a start in the right direction of registering the wealth of material that awaits systematic collection and study. Our texts were located in dozens of books and articles on puns, one-liners, toasts, quotations, aphorisms, and graffiti (see bibliography), most of which are part of Wolfgang Mieder's international archive of proverbs in Burlington, Vermont. The same is true for the many texts based on advertisements, caricatures, cartoons, comic strips, and headlines from magazines and newspapers. The seventy-five illustrations included in our book are just a sampling of the rich iconographic materials of Mieder's proverb archive. Unfortunately we could only include representative examples of this illustrative material, since the printing expenses would otherwise have become exorbitant.

The organization of our more than 3,000 anti-proverbs for 320 traditional proverbs is based on the following pattern: The actual proverbs are arranged in alphabetical order and are printed in bold type. Well-known variants of the proverbs are cited underneath in square brackets. Next we have provided annotations to some of the standard proverb dictionaries, referring to them in abbreviated form with page numbers (see under references in the bibliography). In addition to this pertinent information, we have also included a short statement concerning the meaning of the proverb in round brackets. The anti-proverbs themselves are arranged alphabetically, and for each text we have provided a precise reference. In the case of book sources, only the author's last name, publication date, and page number (except for unpaginated sources) have been registered in parentheses. The bibliography at the end of the book contains complete bibliographical references. In the case of texts from the mass media (headlines, advertisements, caricatures, cartoons, and comic strips), we have cited complete sources in parentheses, including the name of the publication in italics, the date, and the page number. This information will naturally be of help in determining the age of the anti-proverbs catalogued in our collection.

While we have only found two or three anti-proverbs for some well-known proverbs, it is quite normal that we list a good dozen parodies under most proverb headings. But there are also those very productive proverbs which have generated two if not three pages of anti-proverbs, as is true for example in the case of "An apple a day keeps the doctor away," "Early to bed, early to rise, makes a man healthy, wealthy and wise," "If at first you don't succeed, try, try again," "Man does not live by bread alone," "Money talks," "Never [Don't] put off until tomorrow what you can do today," and "The grass is always greener on the other side of the fence." Those proverbs which are built on binary structures have become especially popular formulas on which to base multiple proverb variations, as for example "One X is worth a thousand Y's," "Where there's X, there's Y" and

5

"Different X's for different Y's." Many traditional proverbs are based on such linguistic patterns where the structure is always the same while the image (the metaphor) and the idea (meaning) change. These proverbs belong, of course, to the most popular Anglo-American proverbs, but that is the case in general for all of the proverbs included in this collection. Clearly anti-proverbs can only be effective communicative devices if the traditional proverbs upon which they are based are also known. Otherwise the innovative strategy of communication based on the juxtaposition of old and "new" proverb is lost.

We would like to thank all those colleagues, friends, relatives, and students who have helped us in gathering some of the anti-proverbs included in this unique collection. Special thanks are due Shirley L. Arora, Jan H. Brunvand, Lee and Walter Busker, Barbara and William Busker, Alan Dundes, Katherine Johnson, Isaac J. Levy, Dennis Mahoney, Barbara Mieder, Veronica Richel, George Schumm, Thomas and Jan Schumm, David Scrase, Beverly and John Skinner, Janet Sobieski, Trixie and Eric Stinebring, Rainer Wehse, Beatrice and Jared Wood, and Rosemary J. Zumwalt for having provided mass media clippings for so many years. Many of their "finds" have now been integrated into this collection, making it more representative than it would have been without their much appreciated help.

It might be of interest that both of the compilers of this collection are not native speakers of English. Originally from Russia, Anna Tóthné Litovkina lives in Hungary and is a professor of English at Illyés Gyula Pedagogical College in Szekszárd. Her work on this book has been supported by a Fulbright grant which enabled her to conduct research at the University of California at Berkeley during the academic year of 1998/99. She also received a travel grant from the Jones & Giron Company in Oakland, California. Wolfgang Mieder stems from Germany but makes his home in Vermont, where he is a professor of German and Folklore at the University of Vermont. As Europeans with keen interests in American culture and especially its proverbs,

6

we feel that our collection of anti-proverbs might also be of interest to scholars and students outside of the United States.

It is our hope that this book might generate additional interest in the fascinating world of anti-proverbs from other languages and cultures. Just as traditional proverbs are true "monumenta humana," these innovative texts represent the thoughts, values, concerns, hopes, and yes, joys and humor, of our age as we close out the twentieth century. Our joint efforts toward putting this collection of anti-proverbs together have brought us much joy and excitement, and the fact that a Hungarian and German scholar would put together a book of Anglo-American anti-proverbs can well be seen as a positive sign of international cooperation and friendship.

It gives us much pleasure to dedicate this book to our mentors, colleagues, and friends Professor Vilmos Voigt on his sixtieth birthday and Professor Alan Dundes on his sixty-fifth birthday.

February 1999 WM
ATL

Anti-Proverbs

A barking dog never bites.
[Barking dogs do not (seldom; never) bite].
(DAP 157; ODEP 31; CODP 11-12; MPPS 173; NTC 1-2)
{People making threats seldom carry them out.}
A barking dog never bites
But a lot of dogs don't know this proverb. (Safian 1967: 19)
A barking dog never bites; that is, he never barks while he's
biting. (Safian 1967: 14)
A delivery boy was trying to enter a yard with some bundles but
stopped at the gate because of a vicious, barking dog on the
other side. "Oh, come on in," encouraged the owner from a
window. "You know the old proverb: 'A barking dog never
bites.'" "Yeah, I know the proverb," admitted the boy, "and you
know the proverb. But what worries me is, does the dog know
the proverb?" (Esar 1945: 351)
Remember, a barking dog never bites - while barking. (Metcalf
1993: 63)
Speaking of animals, by the way, I just heard what I think is a
fairly new proverb. It all started when a road hog was squeezing
into the last parking place at the curb. Another motorist drove up
and said, "I'll fight you for it." "Don't be silly," said the other.
"A parking hog never fights." (Howard 1989: 257)

A bird in the hand is worth two in the bush.
(DAP 51; ODEP 59; CODP 22; MPPS 47-48; NTC 2)
{It is better to accept a small, certain thing than to hope to get
a better, larger one.}
A Bible in the hand is worth two in the bookcase. (McKenzie
1980: 43)
A bird in hand is probably contaminated with salmonella. (*The
Burlington Free Press,* June 3, 1995: 1C)
A bird in the hand can be messy. (Reisner 1971: 187)
A bird in the hand is bad table manners. (Adams 1959: 151;
Safian 1967: 34; Metcalf 1993: 141)

A bird in the hand is not to be trusted. (Safian 1967: 34)
A bird in the hand is uncomfortable. (Safian 1967: 34)
A bird in the hand is very bad taste. (Braude 1955: 238)
A bird in the hand is...warm. (Monteiro 1968: 128)
A bird in the hand makes blowing your nose difficult. (Anonymous 1965: 289)
A bird in your hand is worth two in a tree above your new hat. (Esar 1968: 79)
A bluejay in the bush is worth two on a woman's bonnet. (Hubbard 1973: 97)
A book in the hand is worth two in the library. (Esar 1968: 88)
A cadet in the moonlight is worth twelve hundred on parade. (Loomis 1949: 354)
A cock in the hand is worth two in the pants. (*Gent*, January 1984: 26; Mieder 1989: 275)
A girl had in bed is worth two in the car. (DAP 51)
A girl in a convertible is worth three in the phone book. (Safian 1967: 34)
A hair in the hand is worth two in the soup. (Loomis 1949: 354)
A hair on the head's worth two in the brush. (Loomis 1949: 354)
A hug on the veranda is worth two on the dance floor. (Loomis 1949: 354)
A ring on the hand is worth ten on the phone. (Loomis 1949: 354)
A skunk in the bush is worth two in the hand. (Esar 1968: 740)
A thorn in the bush is worth two in the hand. (Loomis 1949: 353)
Englishman: A pound in the hand is worth two on the head. (Loomis 1949: 354)
Maude - "The ring of sincerity was in his voice when he told me of his love.
"May - "It should have been in his hand. A ring in the hand is worth two in the voice." (Copeland 1965: 188)
Nikon Binoculars: Worth all the birds in the bush. (Nikon advertisement). (*Smithsonian*, January 1977: 114)
One girl in the kitchen is worth two at the front gate. (Loomis

1949: 353)
One orgasm in the bush is worth two in the hand. (Reisner 1971:
149)
One spoony girl in the deserted conservatory is worth two in the
crowded ballroom. (Loomis 1949: 353)

A burnt [burned] child dreads [fears] the fire.
(DAP 95; ODEP 92; CODP 32-33; MPPS 110; NTC 2)
{A person who has suffered from something will try to avoid it
after that so as not to repeat a painful lesson.}
A burnt child dreads fire ...until the next day. (Mark Twain, in
Berman 1997: 54)
A burnt child will dread the fire only if it survives. (Feibleman
1978: 126)

A chain is no stronger than its weakest link.
[A chain is as strong as its weakest link].
(DAP 89; ODEP 113; CODP 34; MPPS 104; NTC 3-4)
{Things will break where they are the least secure.}
A brain is no stronger than its weakest think. (Esar 1968: 93)
A flirt is as strong as her weakest wink. (Safian 1967: 35)

A dog is man's best friend.
[Man's best friend is his dog].
(DAP 157; MPPS 174-175)
{A dog is more loyal and faithful to his owner than many people
or other animals.}
A dog is a man's best friend, and vice versa. (Esar 1968: 239)
A dog is man's best friend, especially after you have bet on a
horse. (Esar 1968: 336)
A man's best *Freund* is his *Deutsch*. (Berlitz advertisement).
(*New Yorker*, January 27, 1962: 63)
A man's best friend is his dogma. (Kilroy 1985: 147)
A man's friend is his dogma. (Safian 1967: 43)
Another reason why a dog is man's best friend is because he's
not always calling for explanations. (McKenzie 1980: 140)

If a dog could talk, he wouldn't long remain man's best friend. (Esar 1968: 239)
If my dog could talk, would he still be my best friend? (Yu and Jang 1975: 160)
Man's best friend is his ferret. (*The Burlington Free Press*, June 3, 1995: 1C)
Relax, you won't look wrinkled. "Dacron" is a man's best friend! (Dacron polyester fiber advertisement). (*New Yorker*, April 4, 1962: 83)
The dog is a traveling man's best friend. (Greyhound advertisement). (*Fortune*, May 1971: 19)
The remote control is a man's best friend. (Liu and Vasselli 1996)
The wastepaper basket is a writer's best friend. (Isaac Bashevis Singer, in Berman 1997: 101)

A fool and his money are soon parted.
(DAP 220; ODEP 273; CODP 98; MPPS 236; NTC 6)
{Foolish people spend their money without consideration and soon find themselves without any money at all.}
A fool and her legs are soon parted. (Esar 1968: 638)
A fool and her money are soon courted. (Helen Rowland, in Woods 1967: 283; Safian 1967: 28)
A fool and his father's money are soon parted. (Esar 1952: 202; Safian 1967: 28)
A fool and his home-brew are soon parted. (Loomis 1949: 354)
A fool and his money are soon accepted in the highest social circles. (Berman 1997: 141)
A fool and his money are soon parted, but how did they get together in the first place? (Esar 1968: 513)
A fool and his money are soon parted, but the rest of us wait to be taxed. (Esar 1968: 418)
A fool and his money are soon parted - but they were lucky to get together in the first place. (Safian 1967: 54)
A fool and his money are soon parted, but you never call him a fool till the money is gone. (Esar 1968: 718)

MOTLEY'S CREW

B.C.—By Johnny Hart

A fool and his money are soon parted - especially with the government to expedite matters. (McKenzie 1980: 187)
A fool and his money are soon parted. The rest of us wait until income-tax time. (McKenzie 1980: 186)
A fool and his money are soon parted. The rest of us wait until we reach the supermarket. (McKenzie 1980: 184)
A fool and his money are soon partying. (Esar 1968: 580; McLellan 1996: 81)
A fool and his money are soon popular. (Metcalf 1993: 92)
A fool and his money are soon spotted. (Anonymous 1908: 56)
A fool and his money are...very attached. (Monteiro 1968: 128)
A fool and his money can go places. (Woods 1967: 53)
A fool and his money can make a lot of trouble before they are parted. (Esar 1968: 825)
A fool and his money sooner or later wind up in college. (Loomis 1949: 354; Safian 1967: 57)
A fool and his money, stabilize the economy. (*St. Louis Post-Dispatch*, November 16, 1976: 8D)
A fool and his monkey are soon parted. (Margo 1982: 16)
A fool and his wife are soon parted. (Wurdz 1904)
A man and his resolution are soon parted. (Esar 1968: 677)
A married man and his money are soon parted. (*The Burlington Free Press*, November 17, 1981: 5D)
A miser is the proof that not every fool and his money are soon parted. (Esar 1968: 522)
A mule and its mummy are soon parted. (Farman 1989)
A rich man and his daughter are soon parted. (Kin Hubbard, in Berman 1997: 141)
A widow and her money are soon courted. (Berman 1997: 141)
"Be careful with that coin," he advised. "Remember that a fool and his money are soon parted."
"Yes, Uncle," said Johny, "but just the same I want to thank you for parting with it." (Evan Esar, in Berman 1997: 142)
If a fool and his money are soon parted, why are there so many rich fools? (Berman 1997: 141)
It used to be that a fool and his money were soon parted - now

it happens to everybody. (*St. Louis Post-Dispatch*, January 19, 1975: 12D)

The rich man and his daughter are soon parted. (Frank McKinney Hubbard, in Prochnow 1988: 160)

There was a time when a fool and his money were soon parted, but now it happens to everybody. (Adlai Stevenson, in Metcalf 1993: 119)

They say a fool and his money are soon parted - and the rest of us just wait to be taxed. (Metcalf 1993: 208)

We know that a fool and his money are soon parted, but how did they ever get together? (McKenzie 1980: 187)

We know that a fool and his money are very soon parted, but what would be interesting to learn is how they ever got together in the first place. (Woods 1967: 53)

A friend in need is a friend indeed.
(DAP 233; ODEP 289; CODP 102; MPPS 242; NTC 6)
{A real friend is the one who helps you when you are in trouble.}

A friend in need is a bloody pest! (Kilroy 1985: 202)

A friend in need is a drain on the pocketbook. (McKenzie 1980: 50)

A friend in need is a friend indeed...but friends are for enjoying, not needing. (Berman 1997: 149)

A friend in need is a friend to avoid. (Loomis 1949: 355)

A friend in need is a friend to keep away from. (Benjamin Franklin, in Woods 1967: 345)

A friend in need is a friend you don't need. (Esar 1968: 544)

A friend in need is a pest indeed. (Kandel 1976)

A friend in need is what most of us have. (Esar 1968: 545)

A friend in weed is a friend indeed. (Farman 1989)

A friend that isn't in need is a friend indeed. (Barbour 1963: 99; DAP 233)

A friend with a weed is a friend indeed. (Kehl 1977: 289)

At current prices, a friend in need is practically anybody. (McKenzie 1980: 112)

14

Fair-weather friends
A friend not in need is a friend indeed. (Safian 1967: 48)
It seems that a friend in need is about the only kind a person has
these days. (McKenzie 1980: 191)

A little (bit) goes a long way.
(DAP 379; MPPS 379)
{Small efforts can make a big difference.}
A little courtesy goes a long way, which is just as well since it's
in such short supply. (McKenzie 1980: 114)
"A little goes a long way," as the monkey said when he shat
over the brink of a precipice. (Nierenberg 1994: 545)
A little gossip goes a long way. (Esar 1968: 353)
"A little will go a long way," said the man, as he spit off the
Woolworth building. (Mieder and Kingsbury 1994: 76)
"Well, a little bit goes a long way," as the monkey said when he
shit over the cliff. (Mieder and Kingsbury 1994: 76)

A little knowledge [learning] is a dangerous thing.
(DAP 353, 367; CODP 152; MPPS 366; NTC 10)
{People who know only a little are unaware of their ignorance
and are consequently prone to error or make judgements about
something they are not qualified in.}
A little knowledge is a dangerous thing...and a lot can be lethal.
(Berman 1997: 214)
A little knowledge is a dangerous thing, especially when a child
brings home a poor report card. (Esar 1968: 456)
A little knowledge is a dangerous thing, especially when your
wife has it. (Esar 1968: 203)
A little knowledge is dangerous
Very few of us are apparently out of danger. (Safian 1967: 24)
A little knowledge is not as dangerous as the man who has it.
(McKenzie 1980: 285)
A little learning is a dangerous thing, but at college it is the
usual thing. (Esar 1968: 152)
A little learning is a dangerous thing, but not when the other

fellow doesn't know any more than you do. (Esar 1968: 456)
A little learning may be a dangerous thing - but it's still safer
than total ignorance. (McKenzie 1980: 261)
A little woman is a dangerous thing. (Loomis 1949: 355; Safian
1967: 35)
A little yearning is a dangerous thing. So's a little thing! (Kilroy
1985: 278)
If a little knowledge is dangerous, where is the man who has so
much as to be out of danger? (T. H. Huxley, in Fuller 1943:
177)

A man is as old as he feels (, a woman as old as she looks).
(DAP 396; ODEP 505; CODP 162; MPPS 397)
{Men are judged by their inner youthfulness, women by their
looks.}
A man is always as young as he reels. (Loomis 1949: 355)
A man is as old as he feels before breakfast, and a woman is as
old as she looks before breakfast. (Berman 1997: 258)
A man is as old as he looks before shaving, and a woman is as
old as she looks after washing her face. (Esar 1968: 500)
A man is as old as his arteries. (Berman 1997: 258)
A man is as old as his arteries, a woman is as young as her art.
(Esar 1968: 895)
A man is as old as *she* feels. (Farman 1989)
A man is as young as he feels after playing with children. (Esar
1968: 602)
A man is as young as he feels but seldom as important. (Esar
1968: 304)
"A man is never older than he feels," declared the ancient beau
bravely. "Now I feel as a two-year-old."
"Horse or egg?" asked the sweet young thing brightly. (Braude
1955: 22)
A man is only as old as he looks - and if he only looks, he's old.
(Adams 1959: 170)
A man is only as old as the woman he feels. (Groucho Marx, in
Berman 1997: 258)

A man's as old as he looks when he needs a shave, a woman is as old as she looks just after washing her face. (Braude 1955: 22)
A woman is as old as she looks, and a man is old when he stops looking. (Safian 1967: 16; Esar 1968: 487)
A woman is as old as she looks before breakfast. (Edgar Watson Howe, in Metcalf 1993: 7)
A woman is as old as she looks to a man that likes to look at her. (Finley Peter Dune, in Prochnow 1988: 89)
A woman is as old as she looks until she puts her face on. (Esar 1968: 182)
You're as old as you feel - until you try to prove it. (Safian 1967: 13)

A man is known by the company he keeps.
(DAP 396; ODEP 138; CODP 48; MPPS 397-398; NTC 10)
{You can tell what someone is like by the people that person associates with.}
A careful driver is known by the fenders he keeps. (McKenzie 1980: 64)
A chatterbox is known by the silence she doesn't keep. (Esar 1968: 125)
A company is known by the building it keeps. (U.S. Steel advertisement). (*Fortune*, October 1958: 171)
A company is known by the clients it keeps. (Prudential Insurance advertisement). (*Fortune*, April 1940: 154)
A company is known by the machinery it keeps. (Jarecki Engineering Co. advertisement). (*Fortune*, October 1953: 29)
A company is known by the men it keeps. (Berman 1997: 258)
A director is known by the company he keeps. (Anonymous 1908: 35)
A family is also known by the cars it keeps. (Pierce Arrow car advertisement). (*Fortune*, May 1935: 49)
A girl is judged by the company she keeps - at a distance. (McKenzie 1980: 203)
A good executive is judged by the company he keeps - solvent.

(McKenzie 1980: 164)
A man is judged by the company he keeps, a woman by how late she keeps company. (Esar 1968: 460)
A man is known by the company he keeps, and a woman by the maids she can't keep. (Esar 1968: 720)
A man is known by the company he keeps away from. (Safian 1967: 30)
A man is known by the company he keeps but even better by the company he merges. (Safian 1967: 18)
A man is known by the company he keeps – getting dividends from. (Esar 1968: 181)
A man is known by the company he keeps running at a profit. (Safian 1967: 18)
A man is known by the company he keeps - solvent. (Esar 1968: 104)
A man is known by the company he organizes. (Bierce 1958: 120; Barbour 1963: 100)
A man is known by the company he thinks nobody knows he's keeping. (Safian 1967: 30)
A man is known by the company his wife keeps. (Esar 1968: 161)
A man is known by the company that keeps him. (Esar 1968: 104)
A man is known by the silence he keeps. (Safian 1967: 30; Oliver Herford, in Berman 1997: 258)
A miser is known by the money he keeps. (Esar 1968: 522)
A politician is known by the promises he doesn't keep. (Esar 1968: 639)
A trust is known by the companies it keeps. (Ellis O. Jones, in Edmund and Williams 1921: 455)
A woman driver is known by the fenders she keeps. (Safian 1967: 30)
A woman is known by the company she keeps waiting. (Louisville Times, ca. 1925, in Berman 1997: 258)
A woman is known by the man she keeps. (Hubbard 1973: 137)
"Father, what is it?"

18

"It says here, 'A man is known by the company he keeps.' Is that so, Father?"
"Yes, yes, yes."
"Well, Father, if a good man keeps company with a bad man, is the good man bad because he keeps company with the bad man, or is the bad man good because he keeps company with the good man?" (Edmund and Williams 1921: 202)
It is generally agreed that a man is known by the company he keeps - out of! (McKenzie 1980: 447)
It used to be said that a man is known by the company he keeps but now it's the money. (Feibleman 1978: 17)
Management is known by the company it keeps. (Esar 1968: 501)
Our suit is known by the company it keeps. (PBM clothes advertisement). (*New York Times Magazine*, April 25, 1976: 49; Mieder 1993: 68)
The only man who should not be judged by the company he keeps is a warden. (Esar 1968: 632)
You can always tell real jewelry by the company it keeps. (Ciani jewelry advertisement). (*New Yorker*, September 20, 1976: 18-19)
You can judge a man not only by the company he keeps, but by the jokes he tells. (McKenzie 1980: 277)
You can tell a lot about a person by the time she keeps. (Omega advertisement). (*New Yorker*, May 28, 1979: 81)
Your company is judged by the office you keep! (Cole Steel Equipment advertisement). (*Fortune*, October 1958: 74)

A man's [An Englishman's] home is his castle.
(DAP 304; ODEP 389; CODP 78; MPPS 328-329; NTC 10)
{You can do whatever you want in your own house, no one has a right to enter it without your permission.}
A man's beer is his castle. (Würzburger Hofbräu beer advertisement). (*Boston*, September 1981: 52; *Playboy*, September 1981: 326; Mieder 1989: 274)
A man's castle is his home, and his wife has the keys to all the

rooms. (Safian 1967: 16)
A man's home is his castle. At least that's how it seems when he
pays taxes on it. (McKenzie 1980: 239)
A man's home is his castle - Let him clean it! (T-shirt advertise-
ment). (*Ms.*, March 1978: 100)
A man's home is his tax deduction. (Berman 1997: 197)
A man's home is his wife's castle. (Anonymous 1908: 12)
A man's house is his hassle. (Kandel 1976)
A married man's home is his castle, with him being his vassal.
(Esar 1968: 775)
An Englishman's home is his castle - so let him clean it! (Kilroy
1985: 431)
"How many more times must I tell you, Mildred? A man's office
is his castle!" (*New Yorker*, March 30, 1963: 34)
Nothing makes you feel that your home is your castle more than
getting an estimate to have it repaired. (McKenzie 1980: 112)
To a do-it-yourself, a man's home is not his castle, but his
project. (Esar 1968: 390)

A miss is as good as a mile.
(DAP 413; ODEP 535; CODP 171; MPPS 414; NTC 10-11)
{Almost having achieved something and missing your objective
by a narrow margin is the same as not having achieved it at all
or missing it by a great margin.}
A kiss is as good as a smile. (Loomis 1949: 356)
A miss is as good as a kilometer. (Colombo 1975: 127)
A miss is as good as a male. (Kilroy 1985: 260)
A miss is as good as a mile, but some of them are better at two
miles. (Esar 1968: 234)
A Miss is as good as a Mrs. (Loomis 1949: 356)
A miss is as good as her smile. (Wurdz 1904)
A Ms. is as good as a male. (Abel 1974)

A new broom sweeps clean.
[New brooms sweep clean].
(DAP 72; ODEP 564; CODP 181; MPPS 75-76; NTC 156)

20

{People appointed to a new position or responsibility will tend to inject energy and make big changes.}
A new broom sweeps clean, but an old broom knows all the corners. (Barbour 1964: 292; DAP 72)
A new broom sweeps clean, but an old one knows where the dirt is. (DAP 72)
A new broom sweeps clean, but an old one scrapes better. (DAP 72)

A penny saved is a penny earned.
(DAP 458; ODEP 619; CODP 200; MPPS 482; NTC 11)
{The proverb is given as advice to save even a small amount of money and not to spend it right away.}
A minute saved is a minute earned. (Chemical Bank advertisement). (*New York*, August 7, 1978: 1; *Time*, October 9, 1978: front ad section without pages)
A penny saved gets damn poor interest. (*The Burlington Free Press*, June 3, 1995: 1C)
A penny saved is a penny earned, but it's usually a dollar's worth of time wasted. (Esar 1968: 811)
A penny saved...is a penny out of circulation. (Berman 1997: 320)
A penny saved is a penny taxed. (McKenzie 1980: 496)
A penny saved is a penny to squander. (Bierce 1958: 120)
A penny saved is a penny yearned. (*Boston Globe*, September 23, 1993: without pages)
A penny saved is a pocket burned. (Copeland 1965: 794)
A penny saved...is a political breakthrough. (*St. Louis Post-Dispatch*, November 10, 1976: 8F)
A penny saved is a waste of copper. (Liu and Vasselli 1996)
A penny saved is ridiculous. (Kilroy 1985: 262)
A pfennig saved is a pfennig earned. (Volkswagen advertisement). (*Sunset*, April 1989: 210)
Benjamin Franklin had an axiom, "A penny saved is a penny earned." But that was before the sales tax was invented. (McKenzie 1980: 345)

DUFFY by Bruce Hammond

B.C.—By Johnny Hart

A rolling stone gathers no moss.
(DAP 565; ODEP 682; CODP 217; MPPS 597-598; NTC 13)
{People who do not settle down and constantly move from place
to place will never make money or grow roots.}
A bachelor is a rolling stone that gathers no boss. (Woods 1967:
274; McKenzie 1980: 37)
A closed mouth gathers no feet. (McLellan 1996: 170)
A revolving fan gathers no flies. (Berman 1997: 389)
A rolling football gathers no score. (Safian 1967: 37)
A rolling gait gathers remorse. (Loomis 1949: 357)
A rolling [Stirling] Moss gathers no dust. (*Newsweek*, November
3, 1980: 16)
A rolling stone gathers momentum. (*St. Louis Post-Dispatch*,
November 9, 1976: 8D; Weller 1982)
A Rolling Stone gathers much cocaine. (*The Burlington Free
Press*, June 3, 1995: 1C)
A rolling stone gathers no boss. (Safian 1967: 45)
A rolling stone gathers no moss but gets an elegant polish.
(Loomis 1949: 357)
A rolling stone gathers no moss - neither does it pay rent.
(Loomis 1949: 357)
A rolling stone gathers no moths. (Rosten 1972: 26)
A rolling stone gathers no Mrs. (Esar 1968: 738)
A rolling stone...plays a guitar. (Monteiro 1968: 128)
Always remember,
When at a loss,
That a rolling stone
Gathers no boss. (Rees 1965: 15)
Rolling Stones tickets gather no dust in Utah. (*Salt Lake
Tribune*, September 18, 1994: 10B)
The Rolling Stones are starting to gather moss. (Liu and Vasselli
1996)
The Rolling Stones gather screaming teenagers. (Berman 1997:
389)
There's no easy way to tell you this, Mr. Jagger...I'm afraid
you're gathering moss. (*Express-News*, May 28, 1994: 8A)

24

A soft answer turneth away wrath.
(DAP 20; ODEP 750; CODP 233; MPPS 12; NTC 13)
{A gentle reply to someone who is angry with you will calm the person down.}
A gentle lie turneth away enquiry. (Anonymous 1908: 46)
"A soft answer turneth away wrath," as the man said when he hurled a squash at his enemy's head. (Mieder and Kingsbury 1994: 3)
A soft answer turneth away wrath but has little effect on a door-to-door salesman. (DAP 20)
A soft answer turneth away wrath, but not the door-to-door salesman. (Esar 1968: 696)
A soft dancer turneth away wrath. (Loomis 1949: 353)
A soft drink turneth away company. (Fuller 1943: 95)
"Soft answers turn away wrath," Bill said as he threw two eggs at the bully's head. (Rees 1965: 38)
Teacher was investigating a little altercation. "And what did you do, John, when Thomas called you a liar?" she asked. "I remembered what you said, teacher, that 'A soft answer turneth away wrath,'" replied John. "Why, excellent," approved the teacher, "and what soft answer did you make?" "I hit him with a rotten tomato," said John grimly. (Esar 1945: 18-19)

A stitch in time saves nine.
(DAP 564; ODEP 775; CODP 241; MPPS 595; NTC 14)
{Fixing a small problem right away can prevent serious trouble in the future.}
A drink in time means nine. (Loomis 1949: 357)
A kiss in time saves a nine mile walk. (Loomis 1949: 357)
A lie in time saves nine. (Anonymous 1908: 27)
A pill in time saves nine months. (Kehl 1977: 290)
A stick in time saves nine. (Barbour 1963: 100)
A stitch in time is a surprise to many a husband. (Safian 1967: 35)
A stitch in time means your husband will expect you to wear the rotten old thing year in and year out! (*St. Louis Post-Dispatch*,

November 20, 1975: 8D)
A stitch in time saves a lot of embarrassment. (Safian 1967: 37)
A stitch in time saves embarrassment, maybe. (Anonymous 1961: 200)
A stitch in time saves losing your petticoat. (Anonymous 1961: 200)
A stitch in time saves the day from boredom. (*The Burlington Free Press*, July 10, 1993: 1E)
A switch in time saves crime. (McKenzie 1980: 75)
A woman on time is one in nine. (Safian 1967: 36)

A watched pot never boils.
(DAP 475; ODEP 869; CODP 272; MPPS 507-508; NTC 15)
{Something we are waiting for with impatient attention seems never to happen.}
A watched back door never opens. (*Brattleboro Reformer*, February 16, 1981: 12; Mieder 1989: 274)
A watched cauldron never bubbles. (Mingo and Javna 1989: 195)
A watched clock never boils. (Weller 1982)
A watched pot never boils.....especially if you didn't pay your gas or electric bill. (Liu and Vasselli 1996)
A watched pot never boils...especially when you forget to light the gas. (Berman 1997: 336)
Watched headlights never come. (*The Burlington Free Press*, June 29, 1997: without pages)
Watched pot never gets smoked. (*The Burlington Free Press*, June 3, 1995: 1C)

A woman without a man is like a fish without a bicycle.
(Mieder 1989: 243)
{The proverb is a feminist slogan expressing the independence of women from men.}
A woman without a man is like a fish without a bicycle.
(male response) Yes, but who needs a stationary haddock? (Rees 1979: 80)

26

A woman without a man is like a moose without a hatrack. (Rees 1980: 139)

A woman without God is like a frog without a bicycle. (Haan and Hammerstrom 1980)

A woman's place is in the home.
(DAP 666; CODP 280; MPPS 695; NTC 15-16)
{The stereotypical view that a woman should stay at home, doing housework and raising children.}
A woman's place is every place. (Shaw 1980)
"A woman's place is in the car." (Vinnie Barbarino, *Welcome Back, Kotter*, in Mingo and Javna 1989: 237)
A woman's place is in the delicatessen store and the beauty salon. (Safian 1967: 32)
A woman's place is in the hay. (DAP 666)
A woman's place is in the home because that's where the telephone is. (Esar 1968: 799)
A woman's place is in the home
That's why she's so eager to find a man to put her in her place. (Safian 1967: 25)
A woman's place is in the home
Usually right next to the telephone. (Safian 1967: 22)
A woman's place is in the [White] House. (Junior House clothes advertisement). (*New York Times Magazine*, September 22, 1974: 34)
A woman's place is in the House...and in the Senate. (T-shirt advertisement). (*Ms.*, March 1976: 119; and October 1977: 109; Nierenberg 1994: 551)
A woman's place is in the house...or anywhere else she wants to be. (Trinity College advertisement). (*The Burlington Free Press*, July 22, 1996: 10A)
A woman's place is in the mall. (bumper sticker). (Metcalf 1993: 194)
A woman's place is in the White House. (*Time*, August 6, 1984: 18; Mieder 1989: 275)
A woman's place is sitting on my face. (Nierenberg 1994: 553)

A WOMAN'S PLACE IS IN THE HOUSE.

Even some of the die-hards are beginning to say Amen! Women have finally let their brains come out of the closet because there's an awful lot of mess that needs cleaning up. After all, isn't that what everybody said girls were born to do?

What to wear while doing House Work: Beautiful heathery tones; these in oatmeal and rust, other nice combinations too.
Upper left: Diamond patterned sleeveless sweater over a long sleeve ribbed satin shirt, topped with a diamond cardigan sweater and belted heather bigskirt.
Lower left: A heather duo—the back pleat jacket and belted fully lined trousers joined perfectly with the floral shirt.
Far right: The great sweatercoat, a long sleeve turtle sweater and a sweater-hat. Heather fly front trousers are fully lined.
From $16 to $53 (slightly higher west coast).

Junior House

A woman's place may be with New York Life. (New York Life advertisement). (*Time*, December 5, 1977: 35)

A woman's work is never done.
(DAP 666; ODEP 909; CODP 280; MPPS 398; NTC 16)
{Women are constantly busy with their job or work at home.}
A woman's word is never done. (Adams 1959: 170; Safian 1967: 46; Metcalf 1993: 208)
A woman's work is never done - by men! (Kilroy 1985: 430)
A woman's work is never done, especially the part she asks her husband to do. (Esar 1968: 883)
Woman's day is never done. (*Woman's Day* magazine advertisement). (*Woman's Day*, June 1976: 126)
Woman's work is never done, probably because she can't get off the telephone long enough to do it. (Esar 1968: 398)

A word to the wise is sufficient [enough].
(DAP 672; ODEP 914; CODP 281; MPPS 701; NTC 16)
{Intelligent and wise people can take hints and don't need long explanations.}
A word to the wife is never sufficient. (Safian 1967: 29)
A word to the wife is sufficient - to start a quarrel. (Esar 1968: 653)
A word to the wise guy is unsufficient. (Safian 1967: 29)
A word to the wise is not sufficient if it doesn't make any sense. (James Thurber, *The Weaver and the Worm*, in Thurber 1956: 129)
A word to the wise is - resented. (Esar 1968: 559)
A word to the wise is sufficient, a word to the wife never is. (Esar 1968: 779)
A word to the wise is sufficient...only when the word is wise. (Berman 1997: 455)
A word to the wise is superfluous. (Berman 1997: 455)
A word to the wise is - unnecessary. (Esar 1968: 874)
A word to the wise is useless. (Wurdz 1904)
A word to the wise often gets a very long answer. (Esar 1968:

34)
A word to the wise usually starts an argument. (McKenzie 1980: 12)
To most husbands: A word from the wives is sufficient. (Loomis 1949: 357)

Absence makes the heart grow fonder.
(DAP 3; CODP 1; MPPS 2; NTC 17)
{People feel more affection when they are apart.}
Absence makes some tongues go faster. (Safian 1967: 37)
Absence makes the heart go wander. (Safian 1967: 44)
Absence makes the heart grow fonder, but don't stay away too long. (DAP 3)
Absence makes the heart grow fonder, but presence brings better results. (DAP 3)
Absence makes the heart grow fonder
But presents bring better results. (Safian 1967: 24)
Absence makes the heart grow fonder, but that's not the principle to follow in loving your church. (Esar 1968: 136)
Absence makes the heart grow fonder; distance makes affections wander. (DAP 3)
Absence makes the heart grow fonder - for somebody else. (Anonymous 1961: 200)
Absence makes the heart grow fonder – of the other fellow. (Esar 1968: 2)
Absence makes the heart grow fonder, unless it's our mother-in-law. (Esar 1968: 535)
Absence makes the heart wander. (DAP 3)
Absence makes the mind go wander. (DAP 3)
Absinthe makes the heart grow fonder. (Anonymous 1908: 56; Metcalf 1993: 65)
Absinthe makes the heart grow fonder, and the breath grow stronger. (Esar 1968: 482)
Absinthe makes the tart grow fonder. (Kilroy 1985: 182; Farman 1989)
Abstinence makes the head grow clearer. (Prochnow 1988: 423)

Abstinence makes the heart grow fonder. (Esar 1968: 3)
Abstinence makes the libido grow stronger. (Liu and Vasselli 1996)
If absence makes the heart grow fonder, how some people must love their church. (Prochnow 1988: 431)
Presents make the heart grow fonder. (Esar 1968: 343)

Accidents will happen (in the best regulated families).
(DAP 4; ODEP 2; CODP 1; MPPS 3; NTC 17)
{Nobody, be it a person or organization (often family) is immune from accidents or unforeseen occurrences.}
Accidents will happen in the best regulated families...that's how lots of families get started. (Berman 1997: 2)
Accidents will happen, unless you have an accident policy. (Esar 1968: 433)
Actresses will happen in the best regulated families. (Anonymous 1908: without pages)

Actions speak louder than words.
(DAP 7; ODEP 3; CODP 2; MPPS 4; NTC 18)
{What you do is more important than what you say.}
Actions lie louder than words. (Safian 1967: 39)
Actions speak louder than words - and are just as apt to be misquoted or misinterpreted. (McKenzie 1980: 5)
Actions speak louder than words - and speak fewer lies. (McKenzie 1980: 300)
Actions speak louder than words but not nearly as often. (McKenzie 1980: 5; DAP 7)
Power speaks louder than words. (Dodge advertisement). (*Time*, October 27, 1941: 6)
Sometimes numbers speak louder than words. (Dreyfus equity funds advertisement). (*Wall Street Journal*, June 6, 1996: 3C)
Transactions speak louder than words. (Continental Bank advertisement). (*Chicago Tribune*, April 23, 1991: part III, 7)

All's fair in love and war.
(DAP 14; ODEP 239; CODP 88-89; MPPS 8; NTC 20)
{In some situations, e.g. in amatory or military matters, people
are allowed to use every strategem and take advantage of every
opportunity in order to succeed.}
Airlines: All's war in fares. (*Time*, February 13, 1978: 74)
All is fair in love and golf. (Copeland 1965: 781; Safian 1967:
40)
All's fair in love and competition. (Jones & Lawson Machine
Co. advertisement). (*Fortune*, December 1956: 30)
All's fear in love and war. (Kandel 1976; Kilroy 1985: 262)
All's unfair in love and war. (L.L. Levinson, in Berman 1997:
242)

All's well that ends well.
(DAP 14; ODEP 879; CODP 275; MPPS 9)
{When the outcome is positive, previous failures and disappoint-
ments do not matter.}
All's well that ends. (Kilroy 1985: 426)
All's well that ends well, except in the movies. (Esar 1968: 138)
"All's well that ends well," said the monkey as the lawn mower
ran over his tail. (Mieder and Kingsbury 1994: 149)
"All's well that ends well," said the monkey, contemplating his
beautiful tail. (Mieder 1989: 232)
"All's well that ends well," said the peacock when he looked at
his tail. (Mieder and Kingsbury 1994: 149)
All's well that ends with a good meal. (Lobel 1980)

All roads lead to Rome.
(DAP 513; ODEP 679; CODP 192)
{All efforts will lead to the same result.}
All detours lead to swearing. (Berman 1997: 359)
All public highways eventually lead to a toll booth. (Liu and
Vasselli 1996)
All roads lead to Olivet College. (Olivet College advertisement).
(Pamphlet dated September 1978)

Airlines: All's War in Fares

But rate cuts will not long solve the carriers' troubles

"*The new fares are generating profits and new passenger traffic.*"
—United Airlines President Richard Ferris

"*These fares just generate price wars.*"
—Delta Air Lines Marketing President Joseph Cooper

As in *Rashomon,* the Japanese legend made into a movie, airline executives have widely differing views about the same phenomenon: in this case the spreading cut-rate fares on U.S. and transatlantic flights. What is beyond dispute is that the often bewildering variety of bargains offered by the eleven long-haul lines is stimulating a rush to pleasure travel. That in turn is helping to give the industry a much needed lift.

After years of dismal earnings, the major carriers registered a combined record $600 million profit last year, up from $343 million in 1976. Profits this year are expected by several Wall Street investment analysts to rise to the $700 million area. True, much of the recent increase has come not from flying but from plane sales, tax credits and hotel subsidiaries. Indeed, some carriers—Eastern, TWA, Northwest, Western—show declining operating profits. But the competition for passengers, especially nonbusiness travelers who make up 48% of the traffic, is certain to remain intense. So the number of low-cost fares will probably grow.

Three more bargain plans were

Baedeker for Bargains

The very profusion and complexity of the bargain fares have bothered and confused even the most seasoned traveler. A sampler:

Super Saver, on American, Northwest, TWA and United, for flights from coast to coast and between the East Coast and Arizona, offers from 30% to 45% discounts on basic economy fare. Passengers must buy tickets at least 30 days in advance and stay from seven to 45 days at their destination.

Super No-Frills, on Delta, Eastern and National between New York and Miami or Fort Lauderdale. Fares: Between $55 and $75, depending on the day of the week. First come, first served for 50% of each day's seats.

Super Coach, on American, Continental, Northwest, TWA and United between the midwest and the Pacific coast. Tickets are priced from $99 to $109 with seats limited, but no advance purchase is necessary.

Unlimited Mileage, for travel throughout Eastern Air Lines' system, which reaches from the Caribbean to Mexico and Seattle. The plan is restricted to adult couples (21 or older) at $323 per person, or to an adult with children. Tickets must be bought two weeks before departure, and the itinerary must include three unduplicated stopovers.

Liberty, unlimited travel on Allegheny Airlines' system, which reaches from Boston to St. Louis. Fares: $149 for seven days, $169 for 14 days and $189 for three weeks. Tickets must be bought a week before takeoff, and a three-day minimum stay is required.

proposed last week. Starting March 18, United Airlines will expand its Super Saver plan, which currently knocks 30% to 45% off normal economy fare on coast-to-coast flights. Discounts of 30% to 40% will be available to travelers in all 110 cities served by United for trips of more than 900 miles. American Airlines, the originator of the Super Saver fare, retaliated with an extension of the plan to all 52 U.S. cities that it serves, beginning March 23. Unlike United, American will set no distance requirement.

Meanwhile, Pan American unfurled its "Round the World in 80 Days" fare, which will be offered on a stand-by and reserved-seat basis beginning March 17. Travelers on stand-by will pay $999 for economy class, a discount of nearly 45%, and are permitted eleven stops within 80 days anywhere in Pan American's global network. Passengers with reservations, which must be made 30 days in advance, pay $1,199 and are allowed unlimited stopovers.

The price war on domestic routes is prompted by several factors beyond merely trying to attract new customers. A new regulatory reform bill is now before Congress and stands a good chance of being enacted. Some airline executives fear that it could permit a flock of small, new airlines to enter the market. A number of the established carriers believe that one way to counter such legislation is to prove

All roads lead to romance...with Roman Holiday. (Roman Holiday perfume advertisement). (*New Yorker*, September 29, 1956: 77; and November 3, 1956: 117)
All roads lead to Rome, and all detours lead to profanity. (Esar 1968: 217)
All roads lead to rum. (W. C. Fields, in Berman 1997: 359)
All roads used to lead to Rome. (Lufthansa advertisement for Frankfurt airport). (*Scala*, December 1972: 13)
In the Caribbean, all roads lead to rum. (Esar 1968: 482)
To a romantic girl, all roads lead to Romeo. (Esar 1968: 690)
Well! this is *one* road that doesn't lead to Rome. (*New Yorker*, June 27, 1964: 24)

All that glitters is not gold.
(DAP 256; ODEP 316; CODP 107; MPPS 9-10; NTC 19)
{Superficial attractiveness may not denote great value.}
All that glitters can be yours. (J.C. Penney advertisement). (*San Angelo Standard Times*, February 26, 1984: 11A; Mieder 1989: 275)
All that glitters *is* gold at Chittenden Bank. (Chittenden Bank advertisement). (*The Burlington Free Press*, November 4, 1979: 3A; and December 16, 1979: 4B)
All that glitters is gold. The rest is real wood. (Hallmark advertisement). (*Review*, September 1981: 25)
All that glitters is not brass. (Hubbard 1973: 66)
All that glitters is not gold.
All that doesn't glitter isn't either. (Kilroy 1985: 205)
All that glitters is not gold, nor all that litters, literature. (Esar 1968: 484)
All that glitters - is not Pabst. (Pabst beer advertisement). (*Fortune*, April 1936: 197)
All that glitters is sold. (Mieder 1989: 274)
All that glitters is sold as gold. (*Time*, August 17, 1981: 71; DAP 256)
All that glitters is solid gold. (Dunhill jewelry advertisement). (*Punch*, November 13, 1968: 686)

34

"All that shivers is not cold," said the sea-weary sailor, as he watched the hula-hula dancer. (Loomis 1949: 352)
Gold isn't the only thing that glitters. (DAP 256)

All the world's a stage.
(DAP 677; ODEP 918)
{People and life on this earth are compared to a theater performance.}
"All the world is a stage," and everybody is in a wild scramble trying to get on it. (McKenzie 1980: 102)
"All the world is a stage," and railroad crossings furnish some of the exits. (McKenzie 1980: 2)
"All the world is a stage" and some of us are getting stage fright. (McKenzie 1980: 568)
All the world's a stage, and all the players think they're first-rate drama critics. (Esar 1968: 196)
All the world's a stage, and some women are always rehearsing their woes. (Esar 1968: 835)
All the world's a stage, but most of us are stagehands. (Prochnow 1988: 424)
All the world's a stage, with a lot of bad actors hugging the spotlight. (Esar 1968: 8)
If all the world's a stage, it's putting on a mighty poor show. (Esar 1968: 886)
If "all the world were a stage," our luck would most likely give us a seat on the last row in the third balcony. (McKenzie 1980: 315)
The world is a stage, but the play is badly cast. (Prochnow 1988: 373)

All things come [Everything comes] to him who waits.
(DAP 185, 589; ODEP 231; CODP 4; MPPS 205, 225; NTC 96)
{If you wait patiently you will get what you want.}
All things come to him who hustles while he waits. (Esar 1952: 202)

"All work and no play makes you a valued employee."

All things come to him who waits, but not if he waits in the wrong place. (Esar 1968: 600)

All things come too late for those who wait. (Hubbard 1973: 157)

All things may come to him who waits, but they are apt to be shopworn. (McKenzie 1980: 424)

All tips come to him who waits. (Esar 1968: 813)

Even a waiter finally comes to him who waits. (McKenzie 1980: 449)

Everything comes to him who orders hash. (Safian 1967: 35)

Everything comes to him who waits - except a taxi on a rainy day. (Safian 1967: 16)

Everything comes to him who waits, including the hearse. (Esar 1968: 333)

Good things come to those who weight. (Racquet's Edge Recreation Center advertisement). (*Burlington Free Press*, December 23, 1986: 6A)

Small things come to those who mate. (Farman 1989)

All work and no play makes Jack a dull boy.
(DAP 674; ODEP 916; CODP 281-282; MPPS 701-702; NTC 19-20)
{If you work and don't spend any time on recreational activities, you won't be a balanced and interesting person.}

All work and no Paris? (Air France advertisement). (*Fortune*, September 1964: 19)

All work and no pay makes a housewife. (Esar 1968: 398)

All work and no pay - that's housework. (Berman 1997: 455)

All work and no plagiarism makes a dull parson. (Edmund and Williams 1921: 91; Safian 1967: 46)

All work and no play isn't much fun. (DAP 674)

All work and no play makes Jack a dead one. (Wurdz 1904)

All work and no play makes Jack a dull boy; all work and no spree makes Jill a dull she. (DAP 674)

All work and no play makes Jack a dull boy and Jill a rich widow. (Safian 1967: 32)

All work and no play makes Jack a dull boy - and Jill a wealthy widow. (Esar 1968: 885)
All work and no play makes Jack a dull boy - to everyone but his employer. (Esar 1968: 885)
All work and no play makes Jack a rich man. (DAP 674)
All work and no play makes Jack the perfect corporate drone. (Liu and Vasselli 1996)
All work and no play makes Jack the wealthiest man in the cemetery. (Esar 1968: 119)
All work and no play makes you a valued employee. (*New Yorker*, April 20, 1998: 8)

An apple a day keeps the doctor away.
(DAP 23; CODP 6; MPPS 14; NTC 20)
{Eating an apple every day keeps you healthy.}
A beer a day keeps the doctor away. (*Punch*, February 13, 1985: 62)
A bike [ride] a day keeps the weight away. (*San Francisco Chronicle*, February 2, 1980: without pages)
A compliment a day keeps divorce far, far away. (McKenzie 1980: 97)
A condom a day keeps the doctor away. (Recycled paper Products [Chicago] greeting card purchased in October 1989 in Burlington, Vermont; Mieder 1991: 99)
A crisis a day keeps 'is lordship [the husband] away. (*St. Louis Post-Dispatch*, January 30, 1976: 10D; Mieder 1991: 97)
A crisis a day keeps impeachment away. (Mieder 1991: 98)
A flavor a day keeps temptation away. (Kraft advertisement). (*Better Homes & Gardens*, March 1975: 93)
A fuck a day and you'll never be gay. (Haan and Hammerstrom 1980)
A green apple a day buys the doctor's coupé. (DAP 23)
A joint a day keeps reality away. (Haan and Hammerstrom 1980)
A laugh a day keeps the psychiatrist away. (Esar 1968: 461)
A Mars a day helps you work, rest and play. (Kilroy 1985: 237)
A murder a day keeps the doctor away. (Whiting 1989: 14)

HAVE A HAPPY BIRTHDAY
AND A SAFE NEW YEAR

A patient without health insurance keeps the doctor away. (Liu and Vasselli 1996)
A pill a day keeps the stork away. (Kehl 1977: 290)
A potato a day could keep high blood pressure away. (*Vermont*, Fall 1986: 12)
A slice of pizza a day keeps the doctor away. (*People*, July 27, 1981: 80; Mieder 1989: 274)
An apple a day...could turn the A.M.A. into a fruit conglomerate. (*St. Louis Post-Dispatch*, November 11, 1976: 10F)
An apple a day keeps the doctor away. And so does not paying your bills. (Metcalf 1993: 59)
An apple a day keeps the doctor away; more apples than one keeps him on the run. (DAP 23)
An apple a day keeps the doctor away - unless you get the seeds in your appendix. (Prochnow 1988: 406)
An apple a day keeps the fingers sticky. (Anonymous 1961: 200; DAP 23)
An apple a day makes 365 a year. (Anonymous 1965: 289; DAP 23)
An apple a day puts the dentist to flight. (DAP 23)
An apple a day will keep the doctor away, unless he's a doctor of philosophy. (Esar 1968: 39)
An effort a day keeps failure away. (Mieder 1991: 98)
An onion a day gives your diet away. (Safian 1967: 30)
An onion a day keeps everybody away. (Barbour 1963: 100; Safian 1967: 30)
Apples are so expensive these day, you may as well have the doctor. (Metcalf 1993: 118)
Campbell's Soup.
Better than an apple a day. (Campbell's Soup advertisement). (*Time*, March 7, 1984: 35)
Can a potato a day keep the doctor away? (*Boston Globe* advertisement). (*Woman's Day*, November 1974: 253)
5 miles [of running] a day keeps the doctor away. (Blue Cross, Blue Shield advertisement). (*Time*, November 13, 1978: 31; Mieder 1991: 98)

Can a potato a day keep the doctor away?

If an apple can, a potato can, too. In fact, it can probably do it better. It has more vitamin C. More protein. And more calories.

O.K., knowing this may not change your life. But it might help you plan your meals next week. Which is why we have a daily column called "Nutrition".

It's written by Dr. Jean Mayer of Harvard. It covers all the latest findings and developments on food. And if you've ever wondered how eggs compare with tomatoes or steak with soybeans, it's where you can find out. And finding out might help you eat better for less.

In this day and age, that's food for thought.

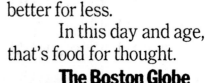

The Boston Globe
We want you to know everything.

Get well soon and remember:
"A Pizza a day keeps the doctor away"
That's "An apple a day keeps the doctor away."
Actually, if the Pizza has lots of garlic on it, it keeps everybody away!
Good grief!
Anyway, get well soon! (Hallmark Card, purchased in December 1977 in Burlington, Vermont)
"I'm worried. My girl is running around with that new doctor in town."
"Feed her an apple a day." (Copeland 1965: 487)
Motto of a Bible-reading family: A chapter a day keeps the devil away. (Berman 1997: 14)
Old Hen - "Let me give you a piece of good advice."
Young Hen - "What is it?"
Old Hen - "An egg a day keeps the ax away." (Copeland 1965: 151)
Read your Bible. A chapter a day keeps Satan away. (McKenzie 1980: 44)

An elephant never forgets.
(DAP 178; MPPS 199)
{The proverb expresses the idea that an elephant with its big head must also have a good memory.}
An elephant never forgets
But what has he got to remember? (Safian 1967: 21)
Elephants and head waiters never forget. (Esar 1952: 202; Prochnow 1988: 432)
They say the elephant never forgets, but what has he got to remember? (Esar 1968: 263)

An eye for an eye, a tooth for a tooth.
(DAP 190; MPPS 207; NTC 21)
{The belief that evil should be returned in equal measure to its perpetrator.}
"An 'aye' for an I," muttered the candidate as he voted for

himself. (Copeland 1965: 785)
When two egoists meet, it is a case of an I for an I. (Copeland 1965: 781)

An honest man's word is as good as his bond.
(DAP 672; ODEP 380; MPPS 699)
{An honest person can be trusted completely.}
An honest man's word is as good as his bond...but many an honest man has a poor memory. It's better to get it on paper. (George Jean Nathan, in Berman 1997: 454)
Many a man is as good as his word, but his word is no good. (Esar 1968: 639)
When a man says his word is as good as his bond, get the bond. (Esar 1968: 883)

An ounce of prevention is worth a pound of cure.
[Prevention is better than cure].
(DAP 482-483; ODEP 646; CODP 207; MPPS 465, 510; NTC 172)
{Taking precautions against something bad is better than repairing the damage after it has already occurred.}
A milligram of prevention is worth a kilogramm of cure. (Colombo 1975: 127)
An ounce of discretion is worth a pound of wit. (Wilson 1970: 601)
An ounce of experience is better than a pound of science. (Whiting 1977: 323)
An ounce of experience is worth a pound of words. (Quaker State Oil advertisement). (*Fortune*, April 1935: 133; Whiting 1977: 323)
An ounce of facts is worth a ton of arguments. (McKenzie 1980: 28)
An ounce of good fortune is worth a pound of forecast. (Wilson 1970: 601)
An ounce of intuition is worth a pound of tuition. (Esar 1968: 439)

An ounce of keep your mouth shut is worth a ton of explanation.
(Mieder 1993: 36)
An ounce of loyalty is worth a pound of cleverness. (Hubbard
1973: 160)
An ounce of mirth is worth a pound of sorrow. (Wilson 1970:
601)
An ounce of mother wit is worth a pound of learning. (Wilson
1970: 601)
An ounce of performance is worth more than a pound of
preachment. (Hubbard 1973)
An ounce of practice is worth a pound of precept. (Wilson 1970:
601)
"Prevention is better than cure," as the pig said when it ran away
with all its might to escape the killing attentions of the pork
butcher. (Mieder and Kingsbury 1994: 100)

Appearances are deceptive [deceiving].
(DAP 22; CODP 6; MPPS 13; NTC 23)
{We shouldn't use looks as an only criterion for assessment.}
Appearances are deceiving, but it's better to have them deceive
for us than against us. (Esar 1968: 207)
Appearances are deceiving: many a girl who puts up a swell
front in public is flat-chested at home. (Esar 1968: 93)
Appearances can be deceiving - a dollar bill looks the same as it
did twenty-five years ago. (McKenzie 1980: 25)

April showers bring May flowers.
(DAP 17; ODEP 17; CODP 7; MPPS 16; NTC 23)
{1. Rain in April helps plants to grow later. 2. Something
unpleasant may lead to something enjoyable.}
Acid rain showers make for dead flowers. (Liu and Vasselli
1996)
April showers bring May flowers...and May showers bring
flooded basements. (Berman 1997: 15)
April showers bring May flowers...but when it's coming down
in buckets, it's hard to think of the goddamn May flowers.

44

(Berman 1997: 15)
April showers bring May flowers, but who wants to wade through mud just to see a bud? (Anonymous 1965: 289)

As the twig is bent, so is the tree inclined [so grows the tree].
(DAP 620; CODP 263; MPPS 652; NTC 39)
{A child's character is molded during early childhood; an adult will behave as taught to act as a child.}
As the prig is bent, so is the snob inclined. (Prochnow 1988: 437)
As the sled is bent, so is the boy inclined; as the slipper falls, so is he made to mind. (Loomis 1949: 357)
Man is inclined as the prig is bent. (Safian 1967: 40)

As you make your bed, so you must lie on [in] it.
[As one makes his bed, so he must lie on (in) it. You made your bed; now lie in it].
(DAP 42; ODEP 502; CODP 161-162; MPPS 37-38; NTC 40)
{You must suffer the consequences of your actions.}
A bachelor is a man who makes his own bed and lies in it - at least a couple of times a week. (McKenzie 1980: 37)
A bigamist is a man who makes his bed and tries to lie out of it. (Esar 1968: 76)
As you have made your bed, why lie about it? (Berman 1997: 25)
As you shall make your bed, so shall you...mess it up. (Stark 1982)
He who makes his own bedlam must lie in it. (Safian 1967: 41)

As you sow, so you reap.
[You shall reap what you sow. As you sow, so shall you reap. As a man sows, so shall he reap].
(DAP 554-555; ODEP 757; CODP 235-236; MPPS 585; NTC 41)
{You must face up to the consequences of your actions and decisions.}

As it snows, so shall ye sweep. (Safian 1967: 45)
As she shows, so shall we peep. (Esar 1968: 232)
"As ye seep, so shall ye row," said the oarsman, as he viewed the punctured shell. (Loomis 1949: 356)
As ye sew, so shall ye rip. (Wurdz 1904)
As ye smoke, so shall ye reek. (Safian 1967: 46; Esar 1968: 746)
Every man reaps what he sows, except the amateur gardener. (Safian 1967: 13)

Bad news travels fast.
(DAP 429; CODP 10-11; MPPS 445; NTC 43-44)
{Negative information spreads quickly.}
Bad news not only travels fast but does so in first class on the evening news and on all the other media airwaves. (Liu and Vasselli 1996)
Bad news travels fast. In many instances, it concerns people who did the same. (McKenzie 1980: 178)
Bad newts travel fast. (Farman 1989)

Beauty is in the eye of the beholder.
(CODP 13; MPPS 36; NTC 45)
{Everybody has a different opinion regarding beauty.}
Beauty is in the ear of the beholder. (Sony advertisement). (*New York*, June 9, 1975: 13)
Beauty is in the eye, arms, legs and back of the beholder. (Mercury advertisement). (*USA Today*, October 28, 1993: 8D)
Beauty may be in the eye of the beholder, but most of us look for it elsewhere. (Esar 1968: 69)
Logic is in the eye of the logician. (Gloria Steinem, in Berman 1997: 23)
"My wife is all in the eye of the beholder." (*New Yorker*, February 1, 1988: 23)

This is our most expensive number. The HP-810. Describing what it has that makes it sound so good requires technical talk. If you know the jargon, read on. Or you can simply listen to it, and hear what we mean.

The HP-810 has components like the acclaimed Dual 1214 changer which operates either automatically or manually. There's a magnetic stereo cartridge with a diamond stylus. And an anti-skating device, which lifts the arm automatically before it can leave a scratch.

And there's an amplifier powerful enough, so if you really want to, you can let all your neighbors know you have Sony's finest compact. Without even inviting them over.

The HP-810's FM tuner has a Field Effect Transistor (FET), which picks up weak signals, yet minimizes interference on strong ones.

Finally, with Sony's acoustic suspension speakers, your ears hear what they're meant to hear. Low lows, high highs and everything in between.

The Sony HP-810. Our very best compact stereo. We don't know how to make it look better. Or sound better.

BEAUTY IS IN THE
EAR OF THE BEHOLDER.

"IT'S A SONY."

Beauty is only skin deep.
(DAP 41; ODEP 38; CODP 13-14; MPPS 36; NTC 45)
{Physical beauty is superficial and may hide an ugly nature, so
don't judge by looks alone.}
Always remember that beauty is only fur deep...feather deep.
(*Burlington Free Press*, May 11, 1982: 7D; Mieder 1989: 274)
Beauty can go as deep as your pockets can...
...just ask any plastic surgeon. (Liu and Vasselli 1996)
Beauty is not only skin deep. (La Prairie Skin Care Collection
advertisement). (*New Yorker*, March 18, 1985: 23)
Beauty is only fur deep. (Mieder 1989: 274)
Beauty is only skin. (Safian 1967: 39)
Beauty is only skin deep, but it's a valuable asset if you're poor
or haven't any sense. (Kin Hubbard, in Esar 1968: 68)
Beauty is only skin deep. But it takes some time to get through
the preliminary enamel. (Anonymous 1908: 15)
"Beauty is only skin deep, but sometimes it doesn't get that far,"
remarked the powder box to the rouge. (Loomis 1949: 353)
Beauty is only skin deep, but the impression it makes is not.
(Esar 1968: 69)
Beauty is only skin deep
This must have been said by a plain person with a very deep
skin. (Safian 1967: 25)
Beauty is only skin-deep, but ugly goes to the bone. (DAP 41)
Beauty is only skin-deep; goodness goes to the bone. (DAP 41)
Beauty is only skin-deep; ugly is to the bone. Beauty lasts only
a day; ugly holds its own. (DAP 41)
Beauty is skin-deep; it is the size of the heart that counts. (DAP
41)
Beauty may be only skin deep, but if she were mine I'd skin her.
(Anonymous 1965: 289)
Beauty skins deep. (Fuller 1943: 29)
Beauty that's more than skin deep. (Olympic stain advertise-
ment). (*Better Homes & Gardens*, September 1979: 17)
Dandruf is only skin deep. (Yu and Jang 1975: 177)
Father - "Remember, my boy, beauty is only skin deep."

Volkswagen was right.
Ugly is only skin deep.

For years, Volkswagen has run great ads telling how the real beauty of their product lies on the inside.

We couldn't agree more.

Which is why we designed our sexy Bradley body to fit perfectly onto a VW chassis.

That way, you wind up with a car that looks for all the world like a $10,000 GT. But inside you still get the famous economy and durability of a VW.

And because our fiberglass body is lighter, the finished product performs better than a stock VW. With top speed increased to 100 mph, and mileage to 35 mpg.

Now, you won't get all this without doing some work. It'll take five or six weekends. But we provide every single part you need and you can do the job with ordinary tools. And you'll find the result well worth your time.

It's a perfect marriage.

The inner beauty of a Volkswagen.

And the outer beauty of a Bradley.

BRADLEY GT

Son - "Deep enough for me. I ain't no cannibal." (Copeland 1965: 214)
I always say that beauty is only sin deep. (Saki, in Esar 1968: 68)
Its beauty is more than skin deep. (Bang & Olufsen turntable advertisement). (*New Yorker*, January 12, 1981: 53; and October 6, 1986: 72 [Rolfs wallet advertisement])
Our beauty is much more than skin deep. (Key-Loc Modular Homes advertisement). (*The Burlington Free Press*, April 24, 1980: supplement without pages)
Paint is only skin deep. (Continental Airline advertisement). (*Fortune*, July 1966: 135)
The difference between them [two suitcases] is only skin deep. (Hartmann luggage advertisement). (*Newsweek*, November 14, 1977: 17; *New Yorker*, November 21, 1977: 190)
Ugliness is but skin deep. (*Punch*, May 5, 1989: 52)
Volkswagen was right. Ugly is only skin deep. (Volkswagen advertisement). (Rowsome 1970: 21; *Sky*, January 1975: 3)

Beggars can't be choosers.
(DAP 44; ODEP 42; CODP 14-15; MPPS 41; NTC 46)
{People in need should gratefully accept what is offered instead of dictating what others should give them.}
Beggars can't be choosers, but some of them seem to make more money than I do after taxes. (Liu and Vasselli 1996)
Beggars should never be choosers - though the beggar often chews what he begs. (Wurdz 1904)
Beginners can be choosers. (Bell Telephone advertisement). (*Esquire*, May 9, 1978: 69)
"You hardly ever see grown-ups using gum. I guess biggers can't be chewers." (*Weekend*, June 17, 1993: 16)

Behind every great [successful] man there is a woman.
(DAP 267)
{Men's careers very much depend on the help of women.}
Behind every beautiful woman, there's a beautiful woman. (Avon

DENNIS, THE MENACE

"YOU HARDLY EVER SEE GROWN-UPS USING GUM.
I GUESS BIGGERS CAN'T BE CHEWERS."

B.C.—By Johnny Hart

advertisement). (*Fortune*, May 1970: 136-137)
Behind every famous man there's a woman - telling him he's not
so hot. (McKenzie 1980: 175)
Behind every good man there's a...good dog! (*Boston Globe*,
August 31, 1997: without pages)
Behind every good moan - there's a woman. (Margo 1982: 16)
Behind every great machine there's a curious mind. (Hayward
Tyler pumps advertisement). (*The Burlington Free Press*, April
8, 1977: 3)
Behind every great man there's an asshole. (Nierenberg 1994:
554)
Behind every great mother stands a man who prodded her along.
(Yu and Jang 1975: 128)
Behind every great woman, there's a man. (Cardin adver-
tisement). (*New York Times Magazine*, March 28, 1976: 8; *New
Yorker*, September 20, 1976: 58)
Behind every great woman there's a man who tried to stop her.
(Kilroy 1985: 266)
Behind every married man there's a woman - and she often
catches him too. (Esar 1968: 425)
Behind every successful man is a wife who tells him what to do,
and a secretary who does it. (Esar 1968: 868)
Behind every successful man is a woman, who didn't have
jewelry, a mink coat, and an expensive home. (Safian 1967: 15)
Behind every successful man is a woman - who hasn't enough
closet space. (Esar 1968: 145)
Behind every successful man is a woman who is trying to keep
up with the Joneses. (Esar 1968: 163)
Behind every successful man is a woman who keeps reminding
him that she knows men who would have done even better.
(McKenzie 1980: 334)
Behind every successful man is a woman who makes it necessary
for him to make money. (Esar 1968: 117)
Behind every successful man is a woman who wanted a mink.
(Esar 1968: 334)
Behind every successful man is one helluva Christmas gift list.

52

(Irv Kupcinet, in Berman 1997: 256)
Behind every successful man stands a proud but surprised wife.
(McKenzie 1980: 480)
Behind every successful man stands a woman and the IRS
[Internal Revenue Service]. One takes the credit, and the other
takes the cash. (McKenzie 1980: 494)
Behind every successful man stands an amazed mother-in-law!
(Metcalf 1993: 149)
Behind every successful man there are usually a lot of unsuccess-
ful years. (McKenzie 1980: 480)
Behind every successful man there's a woman - competing for
his job. (McKenzie 1980: 483)
Behind every successful man there's a woman sneering that she
knows a man who's more successful. (Esar 1968: 161)
Behind every successful man there's a woman - trying to catch
him. (Esar 1968: 117)
Behind every successful man, there stands an amazed woman.
(Metcalf 1993: 205)
Behind every successful woman there is a good man. (*Monterey
Peninsula Herald*, July 22, 1983: 37; Mieder 1989: 275)
Behind most successful men is a public relations man. (Henny
Youngman, in Berman 1997: 256)
Behind every transferred executive stands a woman with a moist
hankie. (Allied Van Lines advertisement). (*Fortune*, May 15,
1969: 224)
Underneath every successful man there's a woman. (Kandel
1976; Kilroy 1985: 262)
"Yeah? Well, there's a woman behind every man that *isn't* a
success, too." (*New Yorker*, February 18, 1961: 129)

Better late than never.
(DAP 360-361; ODEP 54; CODP 18; MPPS 361; NTC 47)
{It is better to do something later than not to do it at all.}
Better latent than never. (Reisner 1971: 145; Yu and Jang 1975:
80; Haan and Hammerstrom 1980)
Better mate than never. (Safian 1967: 35)

53

Better never, from the point of social acceptance, than late at a funeral, wedding, dinner party, or even a businessman's lunch. There are good excuses, particularly good bogus excuses, for the "never," but there is seldom an acceptable one for the "late." (George Jean Nathan, in Berman 1997: 216)
Better never than late. (Anonymous 1961: 200)
It is better to copulate than never. (Robert Heinlein, in Berman 1997: 216)
The widow feels superior to the spinster because even a husband is better *late* than never. (Esar 1968: 460)

Better safe [sure] than sorry.
(DAP 521; CODP 18; MPPS 543; NTC 46-47)
{It is better to be cautious than to do something which you may regret.}
Better SAFE SEX than sorry. (Liu and Vasselli 1996)
It's better to be sure than sorry, but if you're too sure, you're sure to be sorry. (Esar 1968: 785)
'Tis better to be safe than...punch a sixth grader. (Stark 1982)

Beware of Greeks bearing gifts.
(DAP 268; ODEP 250; CODP 78; MPPS 271; NTC 48)
{Be careful from whom you accept favors.}
Beware of a Greek who asks for a gift. (Rosten 1972: 26)
Beware of women bearing gifts: remember Eve. (Esar 1968: 275)

Birds of a feather flock together.
(DAP 52; ODEP 60; CODP 23; MPPS 49; NTC 49)
{People are attracted to others whose tastes or interests are similar to their own.}
Birds of a feather flock together...How can birds flock any other way? (Henny Youngman, in Berman 1997: 31)
Birds of a feather flop together. (Anonymous 1961: 200)
Birds of one feather catch a cold. (Safian 1967: 38)
Do you suppose the day will ever come when birds of every

feather will flock together? (*New Yorker*, August 7, 1965: 25)
People of similar socioeconomic backgrounds flock together.
(Liu and Vasselli 1996)

Blood is thicker than water.
(DAP 57; ODEP 69; CODP 26; MPPS 56-57; NTC 50)
{Relatives have stronger ties and are more loyal and helpful to
each other than people outside the family.}
Blood is thicker than oil. (Nierenberg 1994: 551)
Blood is thicker than water and it boils quicker. (Safian 1967:
13)
Blood is thicker than water
And relatives are always socking each other to prove it. (Safian
1967: 25)
Blood is thicker than water, but sometimes it runs mighty sin.
(DAP 57)
Blood may be thicker than water, but it's probably cheaper than
that natural pure bottled mineral water from the Alps. (Liu and
Vasselli 1996)

Blood will tell.
(DAP 57; CODP 26-27; MPPS 57; NTC 50)
{You can't overcome your heritage.}
Blood will not always tell: it often refuses to speak to poor
relations. (Esar 1968: 669)
Blood will tell: nobody criticizes your faults quicker than your
relatives. (Esar 1968: 669)
"Blood will tell," quoth Macbeth, as he tried to scrub it off.
(Mieder and Kingsbury 1994: 11)
"Good blood will always show itself!" as the old lady said when
she was struck by the redness of her nose. (Mieder and Kings-
bury 1994: 11)

Boys will be boys.
(DAP 65; ODEP 79; CODP 28; MPPS 69; NTC 51)
{Boys are expected to act in a childish way, i.e. be boisterous,

immature, noisy, irresponsible, etc.}
Boys will be boisterous. (Berman 1997: 37)
Boys will be boys and girls will be girls, but not forever.
(Hubbard 1973: 140)
Boys will be boys – and so will a lot of middle-aged men. (Kin
Hubbard, in Esar 1968: 92)
Boys will be boys, but girls these days are running them a
clothes second. (Esar 1968: 93)
Boys will be boys, particularly when they're away from their
wives. (McKenzie 1980: 52)
With today's technology, boys can become girls and girls can
become boys. (Liu and Vasselli 1996)

Brevity is the soul of wit.
(DAP 70; ODEP 84-85; CODP 30; NTC 51)
{Cleverness must be to the point.}
A bright young woman who lives in Buffalo is called Brevity by
her adorer because she is the soul of wit. (Esar 1952: 156)
Brevity is a foreign word to any politician's vocabulary. (Liu and
Vasselli 1996)
Brevity is the soul of wit... and laughter is the goal of wit.
(Berman 1997: 38)
Brevity is the soul of wit - and the sole charm of a bicycle skit.
(Wurdz 1904)
Brevity is the soul of wit – that's why men laugh at fat women
wearing shorts. (Esar 1968: 96)
Impropriety is the soul of wit. (W.S. Maugham, in Adams 1969:
385)
Levity is the soul of wit. (Melville D. Landon, in Adams 1969:
385)

Business before pleasure.
(DAP 75; ODEP 93; CODP 33; MPPS 82; NTC 53)
{You should take care of your responsibilities before starting to
relax and enjoy yourself.}
"Business before pleasure," as the actress said to the producer

when he wanted her to read a script before she relaxed on his couch. (Mieder and Kingsbury 1994: 17)

"Business before pleasure," as the man said when he kissed his wife before calling on his sweetheart. (Mieder and Kingsbury 1994: 17)

"Business before pleasure," as the man said when he kissed his wife before he went out to make love to his neighbor's. (Mieder and Kingsbury 1994: 16)

Pleasure before business. (Thai Airlines advertisement). (*New Yorker*, January 28, 1980: 52-53; Frank Gruber, in Berman 1997: 41)

Charity begins at home.
(DAP 92; ODEP 115; CODP 40-41; MPPS 105-106; NTC 57)
{You tend to take care of people close to you (i.e. your relatives) before taking care of those outside the family circle.}

Censorship, like charity, should begin at home; but, unlike charity, it should end there. (Clare Boothe Luce, in Metcalf 1993: 33)

Charity begins at home and ends on the income tax return. (Esar 1968: 123)

Charity begins at home, and generally dies from lack of outdoor exercise. (Esar 1968: 122; McKenzie 1980: 68)

Charity begins at home and generally dies from lack of out-of-door exercise; sympathy travels abroad extensively. (Fuller 1943: 45)

Charity begins at home and usually winds up in some foreign country. (McKenzie 1980: 68)

Charity begins at home, but that's no reason to treat your wife like a pauper. (Esar 1968: 123)

Charity should begin at home, but most people don't stay at home long enough to begin it. (McKenzie 1980: 175)

Clarity begins at home. (*New York Times* advertisement). (*New York Times Magazine*, January 2, 1977: 35; Mieder 1993: 37)

Indigestion is like charity. It, too, begins at home. (McKenzie 1980: 263)

With home delivery of The New York Times

58

Like charity, obesity begins at home. (Mieder 1993: 36)
Victory, like charity, begins at home. (Warner & Swazey Turret
Lathes advertisement). (*Time*, July 12, 1943: 41)

Charity covers a multitude of sins.
(DAP 92; ODEP 115; CODP 41; MPPS 106)
{Being generous brings forgiveness.}
An autobiography, like charity, covers a multitude of sins. (Mc-
Kenzie 1980: 29)
Charity also covers a multitude of skins. (Esar 1968: 740)
Charity uncovers a multitude of sins. (Esar 1952: 199)
Love covers a multitude of sins - temporarily. (McKenzie 1980:
313)
Psychiatry covers a multitude of sins. (Esar 1968: 644)

**Chickens [Curses, like chickens,] (will always) come home to
roost.**
(DAP 95, 131; ODEP 162; CODP 55; MPPS 108-109; NTC
195-196)
{Your slander or bad deeds will return upon you.}
Chickens always come home to roost, which is right and natural;
but when they come home to cackle and crow, that is another
matter. (Hubbard 1973: 80)
Lies like chickens, always come home to roost. (McKenzie 1980:
301)
The chickens have come home to roast. (Jane Ace, in Prochnow
1988: 1)

Children should be seen and not heard.
(DAP 97; ODEP 120; CODP 43; MPPS 111-112; NTC 58)
{Children should not be obtrusively noisy in the presence of
adults.}
Aural sex should be heard and not obscene. (Kilroy 1985: 280)
Children should be heard and not seen plastered to the TV. (*The
Burlington Free Press*, June 3, 1995: 1C)
Children should be obscene and not heard. (Kandel 1976)

Children should be on scene and not heard. (Kilroy 1985: 241)
Children should be seen and not had. (Safian 1967: 45; Kehl
1977: 289-290; Metcalf 1993: 34)
Children should be seen and not hurt. (Braude 1955: 384)
Children should neither be seen nor heard from - ever again.
(W. C. Fields, in Metcalf 1993: 36)
Fine cars should be seen - but not heard! (Nash advertisement).
(*Fortune*, December 1950: 9)
For those who think sports cars should be seen and not heard.
(Chrysler advertisement). (*Punch*, February 18, 1970: iv)
Graffiti should be obscene and not heard. (Rees 1980: 51)
Highways should be seen and not heard! So make mine new-type
concrete! (Portland Concrete advertisement). (*Fortune*, March
1959: 216)
Humorists should be seen and not obscene. (Loomis 1949: 354)
"Little boys should be seen and not heard," as the boy said when
he could not recite his lesson. (Mieder and Kingsbury 1994: 14)
Manners
Soup should be seen and not heard. (Metcalf 1993: 141)
Pentax sets you free - so children can be seen and not blurred.
(Pentax camera advertisement). (*Time*, November 14, 1977: 40)
The nose is another thing that should be seen and not heard.
(Esar 1968: 553)
When children are seen and not heard it's apt to be through
binoculars. (McKenzie 1980: 69)
Women should be obscene and not heard. (Reisner 1971: 181;
Rees 1981: 96)

Christmas comes but once a year.
(DAP 99; ODEP 123; MPPS 114; NTC 58)
{Good things only come very seldom.}
Christmas comes but once a year, and Christianity comes but
once a week. (Esar 1968: 133)
Christmas comes but once a year, and once a year is enough.
(Esar 1968: 134)
Christmas comes, but once a year's enough. (Copeland 1965:

781)
Christmas comes but once a year
Thank God I'm not Christmas. (Rees 1980: 22)

Circumstances alter cases.
(DAP 100; ODEP 124; CODP 44; MPPS 116; NTC 59)
{If the circumstances change, someone's situation changes too.}
Circumstances alter cases, but in law, cases alter circumstances.
(Esar 1968: 115)
Circumstances alter cases, especially legal cases. (Esar 1968:
464)
Circumstances alter faces. (Safian 1967: 36)
Financial circumstances often alter legal cases. (Copeland 1965:
780)

Cleanliness is next to godliness.
(DAP 101; ODEP 125; CODP 44-45; MPPS 118-119; NTC 59)
{Cleanliness is a great value.}
Cleanliness is almost as bad as godliness. (Samuel Butler, in
Adams 1969: 60)
Cleanliness is godliness, so why go to church? (DAP 101)
Cleanliness is next to godliness, but in childhood it's next to
impossible. (Esar 1968: 142)
Cleanliness is next to impossible. (Loomis 1949: 354)
Cleanliness may be next to godliness, but it is not a substitute.
(McKenzie 1980: 87)
Cleanliness once lived next to godliness, but both tenants vacated
some time ago. (McKenzie 1980: 87)
Cunnilingus is next to godliness. (Reisner 1971: 154)

Clothes don't make the man.
(DAP 103; MPPS 120-121)
{Don't judge a person by appearance and dress.}
Clothes do not make the man. Particularly an apron. (McKenzie
1980: 87)
Clothes don't make the man...but clothes can break the man.

(Berman 1997: 59)
Clothes don't make the man, but it sure helps. (DAP 103)
Clothes don't make the mind. (DAP 103)
Clothes don't make the woman, but they help. (DAP 103)
Clothes don't make the woman, but they often show how she is made. (Esar 1968: 146)
Clothes may not make the man, but they certainly help a woman to make him. (Esar 1968: 146)

Clothes make the man.
(ODEP 16; CODP 45-46; MPPS 120; NTC 59-60)
{You are judged by the way you dress.}
Clothes fake the man. (Berman 1997: 59)
Clothes make the man, and fake the woman. (Esar 1968: 207)
Clothes make the man and it also serves to fake him. (Safian 1967: 18)
Clothes make the man and lack of them the woman. (Safian 1967: 18)
Clothes make the man, and suits make the lawyer. (Esar 1968: 780)
Clothes make the man, except in a nudist colony. (Esar 1968: 555)
Clothes make the man; naked people have little or no influence in society. (Mark Twain, in Esar 1968: 555)
Clothes make the man...uncomfortable. (Berman 1997: 59)
Clothes make the woman and break the man. (Berman 1997: 59)
Clothes make the woman, but seldom is the woman who makes her own clothes. (Esar 1968: 145)
Clothes may make the man, but his backbone grows from childhood. (DAP 103)
Clothes may make the man, but we've seen some where the job still wasn't finished. (McKenzie 1980: 88)
Clothes often fake the man. (Copeland 1965: 790)
The clothes that make a woman can break a man. (Safian 1967: 37)
The clothes that make the woman are the clothes that break the

man. (Esar 1968: 146)
The shirt maketh the man. (Arrow shirts advertisement). (*Punch*, March 4, 1988: inside back cover).

Confession [Open; Honest confession] is good for the soul.
(DAP 111; ODEP 599; CODP 49; MPPS 129-130; NTC 166)
{If you confess something you have done wrong, you will feel better and have mental peace.}
An honest confession is not always good for the soul, but, in most cases, it's cheaper than hiring a high-powered lawyer. (McKenzie 1980: 101)
An open confession is good for the soul, but bad for the reputation. (McKenzie 1980: 101)
Confession is good for the soul
But even more profitable for the psychiatrist. (Safian 1967: 20)
Confession is not only good for the soul; in Washington it can be turned into a bestseller. (McKenzie 1980: 48)
Honest confession is good for the soul but bad for the reputation. (Esar 1968: 168)

Courtesy [Civilty; Politeness] costs nothing.
[Courtesy pays].
(DAP 100,121,472; ODEP 125, 486; CODP 44; MPPS 504; NTC 59, 62)
{It never hurts you to behave in a courteous way.}
Courtesy costs nothing...Try not tipping and see. (*Cynic*, 1917, in Berman 1997: 69)
Courtesy pays compound interest. (Barbour 1964: 293)
Many of the church members had noted that a certain old lady would always bow whenever the name of Satan was mentioned. At last the minister grew sufficiently curious to ask her the reason for it. "Well, Reverend," she answered, "Politeness costs nothing, and you never can tell." (Esar 1945: 70)

Crime doesn't pay.
(DAP 126; MPPS 139)

{Although crime may be profitable for a while, it will not pay in the long run.}
A famous poet was responsible for one of our greatest proverbs. He wrote poetry all day long but was unable to sell it. He sadly remarked, *"Rhyme does not pay."* (Howard 1989: 257)
"As you can see, crime does not pay - even on television. You must have a sponsor." (Alfred Hitchcock, *Alfred Hitchcock Presents*, in Mingo and Javna 1989: 217)
Crime doesn't pay, but at least you are your own boss. (Esar 1968: 193)
Crime doesn't pay, but only if you get caught. (Esar 1968: 193)
Crime doesn't pay, but the hours are good. (Rees 1980: 42)
Crime doesn't pay, except for the writers of detective stories. (Esar 1968: 194)
Crime doesn't pay - or wouldn't if the government ran it. (Esar 1968: 193)
Crime pays - be a lawyer. (Nierenberg 1994: 555)
Crime pays, but you've got to be careful. (Nierenberg 1994: 555)
Grime does not pay. (Safian 1967: 44)
If crime doesn't pay, how come it is one of the biggest business-es in the United States? (Esar 1968: 193)
Nationalise crime and make sure it doesn't pay. (Rees 1980: 42)
Not only does crime pay but it's a straight cash transaction. (Feibleman 1978: 92)
The town loafer had been caught in some petty thievery and was appearing before the judge. "And you want to remember, my man," said the judge as he sentenced him, "that crime doesn't pay." "That may be," conceded the prisoner with a yawn, "but the hours are optional." (Esar 1945: 111)

Curiosity killed the cat.
(DAP 131; CODP 55; MPPS 144-145; NTC 64)
{Curiousity may get you into trouble.}
Curiosity grilled the cat. (Farman 1989)
Curiosity killed the cat, but satisfaction brought it back. (DAP

131)
Curiosity killed the cat,
Information made her fat. (Flavell 1993: 60)
Curiosity killed the cat; satisfaction cured her. (DAP 131)
Curiosity may have killed the cat, but it is what keeps an advertising agency healthy. (Young & Rubican advertisement). (*Fortune*, November 1946: 185)

Dead men tell no tales.
(DAP 138; ODEP 171; CODP 58; MPPS 393-394; NTC 66)
{Dead people will not reveal any secrets.}
Dead men tell no tales, but many have biographers who do. (Esar 1968: 78)
Dead men tell no tales, but their obituaries often do. (Esar 1968: 557)
Dead men tell no tales... which makes it easier for widows to remarry. (Berman 1997: 77)
Many a widow finds it easy to marry again because dead men tell no tales. (Esar 1968: 865)

Diamonds are a girl's best friend.
(not registered in standard proverb dictionaries; but see Rees 1991: 92; and Doyle 1996: 74)
{Stereotypical view of women's interest in jewelry.}
A working mothers's best friend is her Maytag. (Maytag advertisement). (*Better Homes & Gardens*, June 1981: 2)
Diamonds are a man's best friend. (Lippa's Jewelry advertisement). (*The Burlington Free Press*, December 7, 1981: 8A; Mieder 1989: 274)
Diamonds are not a girl's best friend. (Jermoe Alexander Cosmetics advertisement). (*Cosmopolitan*, December 1979: 149)
Did it ever occur to you that aquamarines might be a girl's best friend? (H. Stern Jewelers advertisement). (*New Yorker*, December 5, 1977: 120)

Diamonds Are A Man's Best Friend

See our magnificent collection
of elegantly styled men's diamond
rings of 14K gold.

B.

Charge Accounts Welcome

LIPPA'S

46 Church St., Burlington
Open Mon., Fri. 'til 9, Sat. 10-5

Different strokes for different folks.
(DAP 569; CODP 64; NTC 67)
{People have different interests and preferences.}
Different brutes for different routes. (Chevy Trucks advertisement). (*Outdoor Life*, June 1979: 5)
Different folks, different keystrokes. (*U.S. News & World Report*, October 10, 1994: 109)
Different hopes for different folks. (*Good Housekeeping*, February 1974: 28; Mieder 1989: 327)
Different [ski] slopes for different folks. (Air Canada advertisement). (*Ski*, January 1977: 47; Mieder 1989: 331)
Different smokes for different folks. (*Gallery*, approximately 1974: 114; Mieder 1989: 330)
Different strokes, different votes. (*The Burlington Free Press*, November 1, 1981: 11A)
Different toasts for different folks. (Proctor-Silex toaster advertisement). (*Apartment Life*, December 1980: 105)
Different Volks for different folks. (Volkswagen advertisement). (*Time*, Novenber 25, 1974: 114; and December 16, 1974: 31; Mieder 1989: 328)

Discretion is the better part of valor.
(DAP 152; ODEP 189; CODP 65; MPPS 169; NTC 67-68)
{Caution is better than rash bravery.}
Discretion is the better part of indiscretion. (Esar 1968: 228)
Sometimes the better part of valor is to cut and run. (Berman 1997: 94)
The bitter part of discretion is valor. (Henry W. Nevinson, in Esar 1968: 185)
The coward is always telling you that discretion is the better part of valor. (Esar 1968: 189)

Do unto others as you would have them do unto you.
(DAP 155-156; ODEP 191; CODP 66; MPPS 171; NTC 69)
{The so-called Golden Rule. You should treat others in the same way you would like them to treat you.}

"Different smokes for different folks!"

Do not do unto others what they will not do for themselves.
(Esar 1968: 348)
Do others before they do you. (Barbour 1963: 99; DAP 154)
Do unto mothers. (Mother's Day advertisement). (Berman 1997:
98)
Do unto others and do it fast. (Berman 1997: 98)
Do unto others - and then cut out. (Reisner 1971: 154)
Do unto others as you would have others do unto you - except
do it to them first. (Anonymous 1961: 200)
Do unto others as you would have them do unto you...but better
not expect others to do unto you what you do unto them. (Ber-
man 1997: 98)
Do unto others before they do unto you. (Adams 1959: 170;
Anonymous 1965: 289; Kandel 1976; *New Yorker*, December
14, 1987: 41)
Do unto others what others would do unto you, and do it first.
(Safian 1967: 36)
"How long before they start doin' unto me what I did unto them
others?" (*The Burlington Free Press*, September 13, 1982: 5D)
The golden rule also applies to night drivers: dim unto others as
you would have them dim unto you. (Esar 1968: 348)
Treat others as you would have them treat you -
I can't. I'm a masochist. (Rees 1981)

Don't bite the hand that feeds you.
(DAP 275; ODEP 62; MPPS 284; NTC 49)
{Do not behave ungratefully towards someone who helped you.}
Don't bite the hand that feeds you...or lick the boot that kicks
you. (Berman 1997: 32)
"I always bite the hand that feeds me," as the flea said when it
crawled onto the monkey's paw. (Esar 1952: 80)
The mosquito bites the hand that feeds him. (*Financial America*,
in Prochnow 1988: 403)
The noblest of all animals is the dog, and the noblest of all dogs
is the hotdog. It feeds the hand that bites it. (McKenzie 1980:
140)

Different Volks for different folks.

VW Super Beetle

While most prices have gone up, up, up, the Beetle's has stayed the same, same, same: only $2825* fully equipped.

Station Wagon

Contrary to the headlines, not all mass transportation has gone sky-high. Our station wagon holds up to 9 comfortably and still costs as little as it did a year ago. (And that's a lot less than wagons that hold less.)

70

Don't build your castles in the air.
(DAP 85; ODEP 107; MPPS 94; NTC 52)
{Don't dream too much about unattainable goals and things.}
Build castles in the air
And your psychiatrist will collect the rent. (Safian 1967: 24)
Castles in the air are all right as long as you don't step out of the door. (Esar 1968: 205)
Castles in the air are all right until you try to move into them. (McKenzie 1980: 141)
Neurotics build castles in the air.
Psychotics live in them.
Psychiatrists charge the rent. (Rees 1980: 93)
There are mortgages on every castle in the air. (Woods 1967: 27)
Too many of us forget to put foundations under our air castles. (McKenzie 1980: 141)

Don't burn your bridges behind you.
(DAP 71; MPPS 75; NTC 52)
{Do not destroy all the ways of retreating.}
A pessimist burns his bridges before he gets to them. (McKenzie 1980: 196)
A pessimist is a man who burns all his bridges in front of him. (Metcalf 1993: 163)
Don't burn your bridges behind you...unless you're sure you can swim. (Berman 1997: 39)

Don't change [swap] horses in midstream [while crossing a stream; at the middle of the stream].
(DAP 311; ODEP 791; CODP 40; MPPS 325; NTC 70)
{Don't change direction or tactics when you are in the middle of doing something.}
Don't change houses in mid dream. (Farman 1989)
Don't swap horses while crossing a stream...nor ever change diapers in midstream. (Berman 1997: 196)
One of the most important things to remember about infant care

is: Never change diapers in midstream. (Don Marquis, in Esar 1968: 423)

Don't count your chickens before they are hatched [hatch].
(DAP 95; ODEP 147; CODP 50-51; MPPS 109; NTC 70)
{Don't be overconfident and too optimistic that something will happen, and never assume success before things have turned out favorably for you.}
Don't count your boobies until they are hatched. (James Thurber, *The Unicorn in the Garden*, in Thurber 1940: 66)
Don't count your U.S. Air jets before they land. (Liu and Vasselli 1996)
Don't enumerate your fowl until the process of incubation has materialized. (Anonymous 1965: 289)

Don't cross the bridge till you come to it.
[Don't cross your bridges before you come to them].
(DAP 71; ODEP 156; CODP 32; MPPS 74-75; NTC 63)
{Don't worry about something until it has happened.}
Don't cross a bridge before it's built. (Berman 1997: 39)
Don't cross your bridges before you consult your dentist. (DAP 71)
Don't try to cross any bridges until you're sure one is there. (McKenzie 1980: 64)
The man who crosses his bridges before he gets to them is probably following a road map. (Esar 1968: 502)
When we come to that bridge, we'll jump off it. (Rosten 1972: 32)

Don't cry [(It's) No use crying] over spilt milk.
(DAP 410; ODEP 159; CODP 54; MPPS 411; NTC 127)
{Don't get upset about something that has already happened and can't be changed.}
If you must cry over spilt milk, condense it. (Esar 1968: 517)
Never cry over spilt milk. It could've been whiskey. (Mingo and Javna 1989: 24)

No use crying over spilt milk
But what about the burned toast and the weak coffee? (Safian
1967: 22)
Philosopher - One who instead of crying over spilt milk consoles
himself with the thought that it was over four-fifths water.
(Copeland 1965: 772)

Don't kick [hit] a man [fellow] when he's down.
(DAP 205; ODEP 374; MPPS 401)
{Don't hurt someone who is at a disadvantage}
Kickin' a man when he's down sometimes is the only way to
make him get up. (Alstad 1992: 19)
Never kick a man when he's down - he may get up. (Safian
1967: 14)
Never kick a man when he's down, unless you're sure he's not
going to get up again. (Esar 1968: 306)
One young man was sitting on another's chest outside a pub,
with his fist upraised. Just then a woman came out of the pub.
'Wait!' she cried. 'You wouldn't hit a man when he was down,
would you?'
And the man on top said, 'What do you think I got him down
for?' (Metcalf 1993: 81)

Don't make a mountain out of a molehill.
(DAP 419; ODEP 547; MPPS 428; NTC 145)
{Don't exaggerate.}
A gossip usually makes a mountain out of a molehill by adding
some dirt. (Esar 1968: 536)
After the election, the successful candidates start making
molehills out of the mountains they erected. (Esar 1968: 261)
It isn't difficult to make a mountain out of a molehill - just add
a little dirt. (McKenzie 1980: 161)
Molehills of debt build mountains of worry. (McKenzie 1980:
125)
My wife's hobby is making things - like mountains out of
molehills. (Metcalf 1993: 12)

Never make a mountain out of a mole-hill -Try gold, silver, copper or radium - there's more in it. (Wurdz 1904)
The wife who makes a mountain out a molehill probably has a husband who makes a molehill out of a mountain. (Esar 1968: 278)
Ulcers are things you get from making mountains out of molehills. (Berman 1997: 293)
When you make a mountain out of a molehill, don't expect anyone to climb up to see the view. (McKenzie 1980: 160)

Don't put all your eggs in one basket.
(DAP 177; ODEP 218; CODP 75; MPPS 198; NTC 71)
{Do not risk everything on one single venture.}
A family of Basques got caught in a revolving door. The moral? Don't put all your Basques in one exit. (Anonymous 1961: 200)
Don't put all your chickens in one basket. (Rosten 1972: 28)
Don't put all your eggs in one basket, or all your whiskey in one guest. (Esar 1968: 362)
Don't put all your eggs in one basket - try an incubator. (Wurdz 1904)
Don't put all your eggs in one basket, unless you're at the supermarket. (Esar 1968: 783)
Don't put all your eggs in one nog. (Paul Masson champagne advertisement). (*New Yorker*, December 13, 1958: 133)
Don't put all your money into one stock. (Liu and Vasselli 1996)
Easter is the only time when it's perfectly safe to put all your eggs in one basket. (Esar 1968: 252)
Put all your eggs where nobody can step on 'em. (*The Burlington Free Press*, January 5, 1992: without pages)

Early to bed, early to rise, makes a man healthy, wealthy and wise.
(DAP 42; ODEP 211; CODP 73; MPPS 37; NTC 74)
{The proverb is given as medical advice for healthy living.}
Early to bed and early to rise - and it probably means your TV set is being repaired. (Safian 1967: 32)

Early to bed and early to rise - and it's a sure sign that you don't care for the Late, Late Shows. (Safian 1967: 32)

Early to bed and early to rise, and you'll be in a tax bracket up to the skies. (Esar 1968: 418)

Early to bed and early to rise - and you'll miss some of the most interesting people. (Safian 1967: 32)

Early to bed and early to rise - and you'll never see red in the whites of your eyes. (Safian 1967: 32)

Early to bed and early to rise, and you'll never show red in the whites of your eyes. (Esar 1952: 251)

Early to bed and early to rise - and you'll remain an unskilled employee. (Safian 1967: 32)

Early to bed and early to rise, and your head will not feel seven times its own size. (Esar 1952: 251)

Early to bed and early to rise, and your girl will go out with additional guys. (Esar 1952: 251)

Early to bed and early to rise - and your neighbors will wonder why you can't get a job with better hours. (Safian 1967: 32)

Early to bed and early to rise - doesn't make a girl a friend of the guys. (Safian 1967: 32)

Early to bed and early to rise...gives a guy reason for hiding his eyes. (*St. Louis Post-Dispatch*, November 13, 1976: 4B)

Early to bed and early to rise is the best way to read the morning paper in peace and quiet. (Esar 1968: 250)

Early to bed and early to rise is the curse of the working class. (Mingo and Javna 1989: 247)

Early to bed and early to rise is the way of a girl before she gets wise. (Esar 1968: 250)

Early to bed and early to rise is the way of teenagers before they get wise. (Esar 1952: 251)

Early to bed and early to rise, makes a man a farmer! (Wurdz 1904)

Early to bed and early to rise makes a man get his own breakfast. (Esar 1968: 95)

Early to bed and early to rise makes a man...not watch T.V. (Monteiro 1968: 128)

"HOW LONG BEFORE THEY START DOIN' UNTO ME WHAT I DID UNTO THEM OTHERS ?"

"Remember this: early to bed, early to rise, work like hell and computerise."

Early to bed and early to rise makes you the kind party-givers despise. (Esar 1968: 250)
Early to bed and early to rise - or the boss'll promote the other guys. (*Boston Herald*, January 2, 1959: 16)
Early to bed and early to rise probably indicates unskilled labor. (John Giardi, in Esar 1968: 264)
Early to bed, early to rise and you never meet any prominent people. (George Ade, in Mieder 1993: 126; Carl Sandburg, *Good Morning, America*, in Mieder 1993: 118)
Early to bed, early to rise makes sure you get out before her husband arrives. (Mieder 1993: 124)
Early to bed, early to rise - makes you healthy, but socially a washout. (Safian 1967: 32)
Early to bed, early to rise, moderate exercise. (Mieder 1993: 110)
Early to bed and early to rise,
Never get tight, and advertise. (Loomis 1949: 353)
Early to bed and late to rise and you wear what belongs to the other guys. (Loomis 1949: 353)
Early to bed, early to rise
And your girl goes out with other guys. (Loomis 1949: 353)
Early to bed, early to rise: dull isn't it? (Anonymous 1965: 289)
Early to bed, early to rise
Will make you miss all regular guys. (George Ade, in Mieder 1993: 118)
Early to bed.
Early to rise.
Work like hell
and advertise.
(Kate Harper Designs greeting card purchased in April 1996 in Berkeley, California)
Early to bid and early to raise makes a poor bridge player. (Safian 1967: 46)
Early to rise and early to bed makes a girl healthy but socially dead. (Esar 1952: 251)
Early to rise and early to bed makes a male healthy and wealthy

and dead. (James Thurber, *The Shrike and the Chipmunks*, in Thurber 1940: 22)

Late to bed and early to rise, and you'll have dark rings under your eyes. (Esar 1952: 251; Safian 1967: 33)

Late to bed and early to rise, and your head will feel five times its size. (Safian 1967: 33)

Late to bed, late to rise, who in the hell wants to be wise? (Loomis 1949: 353)

Nowadays early to bed and early to rise probably means the television set isn't working. (Esar 1968: 250)

On your birthday...
...if you're not interested in being healthy, wealthy, and wise...
...how about early to bed?!
Have a happy day. (Mark I, Inc. [Chicago, Illinois] greeting card, purchased in November 1980 in Chicago; Mieder 1993: 125)

"Remember this: early to bed, early to rise, work like hell and computerise." (*Punch*, January 13, 1989: 15)

Eat, drink, and be merry (, for tomorrow we may die).
(DAP 175; MPPS 195; NTC 75-76)
{Enjoy your life as much as possible, because you may die soon.}

Carousers

Eat, drink and be merry, and tomorrow you'll wish you were dead. (Safian 1967: 48)

"Eat, drink, and be merry, for tomorrow the cook leaves," as the fellow says. (Mieder and Kingsbury 1994: 38)

Eat, drink and be merry for tomorrow they may not be deductible. (Esar 1968: 283)

Eat, drink and be merry for tomorrow they may recall your credit cards. (Berman 1997: 110)

Eat, drink, and be merry, for tomorrow ye diet. (Safian 1967: 43)

Eat, drink and be merry for tomorrow you may be radioactive.

(Reisner 1971: 126)
Eat, drink and be merry, for tomorrow you may diet. (Anonymous 1965: 289)
Eat, drink, and be merry, for tomorrow you may not be able to afford it. (Esar 1968: 332)
Eat, drink, and be merry, for tomorrow your wife may come home. (DAP 175)
Eat, drink, and be mystified. (Caesars Palace advertisement). (*Hemispheres*, June 1997: 16)
Eat, drink and be varied. (Stieff pewter advertisement). (*New Yorker*, May 16, 1977: 57; and May 5, 1980: 121)
Nowadays when a girl goes out on a blind date, she should eat, drink and be wary. (Esar 1968: 118)
Tim's Gay bar
Eat, Drink and be Mary. (*Playboy*, May 1975: 170)
Tipplers
Eat, drink, and be carried. (Safian 1967: 47)

Even a worm will turn.
[The worm will turn].
(DAP 679; ODEP 837; CODP 282-283; MPPS 705; NTC 77)
{Even weak people will rise up if hurt too much.}
A henpecked husband is the only species of worm that's afraid to turn. (Esar 1968: 381)
When the worm turns, that is all it accomplishes. (Esar 1968: 5)

Every cloud has a silver lining.
(DAP 104; ODEP 128; CODP 46; MPPS 121; NTC 77-78)
{Every misfortune or difficult circumstance has its bright side. One should be optimistic even in the most desperate situation.}
A farmer had been moaning to a friend about adverse farming conditions until finally the friend objected, "It's not that bad, Hi. Remember, every cloud's got a silver lining" "Humph!" grunted Hiram. "It'd be better if they had an arsenic linin' then when it rained it'd spray the crops with bug-killer as well as water 'em." (Esar 1945: 85)

A pessimist is someone who sees a cloud in every silver lining. (Metcalf 1993: 163)
"Behind every dark cloud, there's usually rain." (Mike Nesmith, in Mingo and Javna 1989: 116)
Behind every silver lining there's a dark cloud. (Kehl 1977: 290)
Every cloud has a silver lining...But not the kind of silver you can take to the bank. (Berman 1997: 60)
Every cloud has a silver lining: when you get a divorce, you also get rid of your mother-in-law. (Esar 1968: 534)
Every silver lining has a cloud around it. (Rosten 1972: 28)
To the pickpocket, every crowd has a silver lining. (Berman 1997: 61)
To the undertaker, every shroud has a silver lining. (Berman 1997: 61)

Every dog has his day.
(DAP 159; ODEP 195; CODP 67; MPPS 175; NTC 78)
{Fortune smiles at least once in a lifetime on everyone.}
Every dog has his day, and the cats their nights. (DAP 159)
Every dog may have his day, but it's the puppies that have weak ends. (Esar 1968: 239)
Every dogma has its day. (Safian 1967: 41)
Every dogma must have its day. (Esar 1968: 239)

Every little (bit) helps.
(DAP 379; ODEP 228; CODP 79; MPPS 379)
{Little by little you can gain much.}
"Every little bit helps," as the old lady said when she pissed in the ocean to help drown her husband. (Mieder and Kingsbury 1994: 76)
"Every little bit helps," as the old woman said when she spit in the cistern. (Mieder 1989: 237)
Every little bit helps, but it only helps a little bit. (Esar 1968: 380)
"Every little bit helps," said the old fisherman to his wife, as he threw the fish net on the bed on a cold winter night. (Mieder and

Kingsbury 1994: 76)
"Every little helps," as the captain said when he threw his wife
overboard to lighten the ship. (Mieder and Kingsbury 1994: 75)
"Every little helps," as the old woman said when she beat up a
dead fly in her currant cake. (Mieder and Kingsbury 1994: 76)
"Every little helps," quoth the wren when she pissed in the sea.
(Mieder and Kingsbury 1994: 75)
"Every little helps," said Mr. Little and took the six little Littles
out to help him saw a pile of wood. (Mieder and Kingsbury
1994: 76)

Every man for himself.
(DAP 398; ODEP 229; CODP 79-80; MPPS 394; NTC 79)
{People have to fight for their own survival.}
"Every man for himself," as the jackass said when he stamped
among the young turkies. (Mieder and Kingsbury 1994: 82)
Her motto is, 'Every man for myself.' (Metcalf 1993: 93)

Every man has his price.
(DAP 399; ODEP 229; CODP 80; MPPS 395; NTC 79)
{Everyone can be bribed, provided the bribe is big enough.}
Every man has his price, and every woman has her figure. (Esar
1968: 499)
Every man has his price...and you're an unbelievable bargain.
(Berman 1997: 256)
Every man has his price, but brides are given away. (Esar 1968:
96)
Every man has his price, but some hold bargain sales. (Edmund
and Williams 1921: 216)
Every man has his price...Make me an offer. (Berman 1997:
256)
Every politician has his price, especially those who are worth-
less. (Esar 1968: 614)

Every man [Everyone; Everybody] to his (own) taste.
(DAP 399; ODEP 230; CODP 81; MPPS 395-396; NTC 79-80)

{People have the right to find their own satisfaction.}
"Everyone to her own taste," as the old lady said when she kissed the pig. (Mieder and Kingsbury 1994: 134)
"Everyone to his own taste," as the farmer said when he kissed the cow. (Mieder and Kingsbury 1994: 134)
"Everyone to their own taste," as the cow said when she rolled in the pig pen. (Mieder and Kingsbury 1994: 135)

Everybody's business is nobody's business.
(DAP 76; ODEP 231; CODP 82)
{People should mind their own affairs.}
Everybody's business is nobody's business, except the busybody's. (Esar 1968: 511)
Nobody's business is everybody's curiosity. (Esar 1968: 200)
What's everybody's business is nobody's business except the journalist's. (Joseph Pulitzer, in Berman 1997: 41)

Experience is the best teacher.
(DAP 189; CODP 85; MPPS 207; NTC 81)
{You learn best through practice.}
Expedience is the best teacher. (Kandel 1976)
Experience is the best teacher, but the tuition is much too high. (Esar 1968: 285)
Experience may be the best teacher, but she's not the prettiest. (McKenzie 1980: 167)
If experience is the best teacher, how is it that some husbands still think they're the boss of the family? (McKenzie 1980: 166)

Faint heart never won fair lady.
(DAP 292; ODEP 238; CODP 88; MPPS 298; NTC 82)
{Courage leads to great achievements, especially in courting women.}
Faint heart ne'er won a mother-in-law. (Esar 1952: 220)
Faint heart ne'er won fair lady - without plenty of help on her part. (Esar 1968: 187)
Faint heart ne'er won fur, lady. (Safian 1967: 43)

Faint heart never won fair lady, and neither did faint praise.
(Esar 1968: 624)
Faint heart never won fair lady...but a faint whisper often
catches her. (Berman 1997: 184)
Faint heart never won fair lady - but a full purse can always pull
the trick. (Wurdz 1904)
Faint heart never won fair lady, nor dark one either. (Esar 1968:
733)
Faint heart never won fair lady or a fat turkey. (Barbour 1964:
295)
Faint heart never won fair lady, or escaped one either. (Esar
1968: 733)
Faint praise ne'er won fair lady. (Esar 1968: 313)

Faith will [can] move mountains.
(DAP 196; CODP 89; NTC 82)
{Your faith and belief in what you are doing will help you to
overcome any obstacle.}
Doubt makes the mountain which faith can move. (McKenzie
1980: 173)
Faith can move mountains - she's a big girl. (Rees 1981: 50)
Faith either moves mountains or tunnels through. (McKenzie
1980: 174)
Faith may move mountains, but it takes work to tunnel them.
(Esar 1968: 536)
Faith will move mountains... but not furniture. (Berman 1997:
131)
I'm just moving clouds today - tomorrow I'll try mountains.
(Ashleigh Brilliant, in Berman 1997: 131)
If your faith cannot move mountains, it ought to at least climb
them. (McKenzie 1980: 174)

Familiarity breeds contempt.
(DAP 198; ODEP 243; CODP 89-90; MPPS 213; NTC 83)
{The better we know someone or something, the more likely it
is that our respect will degenerate into disregard.}

A president likes to keep on good terms with the press corps because unfamiliarity breeds contempt. (Berman 1997: 132)
Familiarity breeds. (Safian 1967: 27; Kilroy 1985: 277)
Familiarity breeds attempt. (Anonymous 1961: 200; Safian 1967: 27)
Familiarity breeds consent. (Berman 1997: 132)
Familiarity breeds contempt - and children. (Mark Twain, in Myers 1968: 47; DAP 198)
Familiarity breeds contempt...and self-contempt breeds contempt for others. (Berman 1997: 132)
Familiarity breeds content. (Safian 1967: 27)
Familiarity breeds... lust. (Kandel 1976)
Family tea breeds contempt. (Kilroy 1985: 136)
In politics, familiarity breeds votes. (Esar 1968: 109)

Feed [Stuff] a cold and starve a fever.
(DAP 106; ODEP 783; CODP 92; MPPS 126; NTC 83)
{Eating will help cure a cold, withholding food will help cure a fever.}
Feed a cold, feed a fever. (Mieder 1991: 96)
Feed a fever, feed a cold. (*The Burlington Free Press*, January 28, 1987: 2D)
Flood a cold and drown a fever. (*St. Louis Post-Dispatch*, September 13, 1974: 12D; Mieder 1991: 96)
Is it "Feed a cold and starve a fever" or the other way round? You're asking old "Feed a fever, feed a cold?" (*The Burlington Free Press*, September 22, 1983: 11D)

Figures don't lie.
(DAP 207; MPPS 222)
{Statistics can prove anything.}
Figures don't lie, but a girdle condenses the truth. (Safian 1967: 14)
Figures don't lie, but liars figure. (Esar 1968: 307)
Figures don't lie - except on the beach. (Esar 1968: 67)
Statistician: A liar who can figure. (Woods 1967: 34)

Fine feathers make fine birds.
(DAP 204; ODEP 258; CODP 94; MPPS 217-218; NTC 85)
{Good appearance and dress might indicate a good character.}
Fine feathers make fine birds...extinct. (Berman 1997: 134)
Fine feathers make fine birds...No! Fine birds make fine
feathers. (Berman 1997: 134)
Fine feathers make fine birds...until it comes time to fly.
(Mignon McLaughlin, in Berman 1997: 134)
Fine feathers make fine feather-beds. (Wurdz 1904)

Fools rush in where angels fear to tread.
(DAP 222-223; CODP 100; MPPS 236-237; NTC 87)
{Foolish people act hastely and attempt feats that wise people
would avoid.}
Fools run in where fools have been before. (McLellan 1996: 81)
Fools rush in and take the best seats. (Berman 1997: 144)
Fools rush in where angels wouldn't even send a calling card.
(McKenzie 1980: 186)
Fools rush in where wise men fear to trade. (Esar 1968: 104)
Widows rush in where spinsters fear to tread. (Esar 1968: 865)

Forgive and forget.
(DAP 228-229; ODEP 281; MPPS 239; NTC 88)
{Not only forgive someone but put out of mind all wrongs ever
caused to you by that person.}
A woman may promise to forgive and forget, but she will never
promise to forget she has forgiven. (Esar 1968: 324)
But you promised to forgive and forget!
Yes, but I don't want you to forget that I've forgiven and
forgotten! (Metcalf 1993: 13)
I'll forgive and I'll forget, but I'll remember. (Slung 1986: 11)
We should forgive and then forget what we have forgiven.
(McKenzie 1980: 188)

Gentlemen prefer blondes.
(DAP 249; MPPS 250)

86

{A sterotypical male view of women.}
According to the tobacco ads, gentlemen prefer blends. (Esar
1968: 137)
Blondes prefer gentlemen with money. (Safian 1967: 39)
Gentlemen be-fur blondes. (Safian 1967: 44)
Gentlemen prefer blondes but it isn't always mutual. (Esar 1952:
199)

**Give a man [someone; him] enough rope and he will hang
himself.**
(DAP 400; ODEP 683; CODP 218; MPPS 537; NTC 93)
{Given the opportunity and freedom to behave badly, people will
bring about their own downfall.}
Give a boss with a sexy secretary enough rope, and he's bound
to be tied up at the office. (Safian 1967: 30)
Give a convict enough rope and he'll skip. (Copeland 1965: 781)
Give a girl enough rope and she'll ring the wedding bell.
(McKenzie 1980: 202)
Give a housewife enough rope and she'll make macramé hangers
for all her houseplants. (Berman 1997: 360)
Give a husband enough rope, and he'll want to skip. (Woods
1967: 295; Safian 1967: 30)
Give a man enough hope and he'll hang himself. (Kandel 1976)
Give a man enough rope and he skips; give a woman enough
rope, and she makes a marriage knot. (Esar 1968: 692)
Give a man enough rope, and he'll hang himself; give a woman
enough rope, and she'll want pearls on it. (Esar 1968: 587)
Give a man enough rope and he'll hang you. (Rosten 1972: 26;
Kilroy 1985: 164)
Give a quack enough rope and he'll hang up a shingle. (McKen-
zie 1980: 397)
Give a thief enough rope and he'll tie up the night watchman.
(Berman 1997: 360)
Give a woman enough rope, and she'll hang another clothes-line
in the bathroom. (Safian 1967: 30)
Give an enterprising fellow enough rope and he'll go into the

rope business. (Berman 1997: 360)
Give him enough rope - and he'll skip. (Kilroy 1985: 425)

Give him an inch and he'll take an ell [a yard].
(DAP 328; ODEP 303; MPPS 336; NTC 92-93)
{If you are kind and generous to someone, the person will take
advantage of you and will demand more.}
Give a chiropodist an inch, and he will take a foot. (Esar 1968:
304)
Give a chiropodist an inch, and he'll take the whole foot. (Safian
1967: 29)
Give a husband an inch, and it's all the closet space he'll get.
(Safian 1967: 29)
Give a motorist an inch and he'll take off one of your fenders.
(McKenzie 1980: 142)
Give a pedestrian an inch and he'll take a chance. (McKenzie
1980: 387)
Give a skeptic an inch, and he'll measure it. (Esar 1968: 739)
Give a woman a pinch, and she'll buy the shoe. (Safian 1967:
29)
Give a woman an inch, and he thinks he's a ruler. (Anonymous
1965: 290)
Give a woman an inch, and she'll complain that nothing fits her
anymore. (Safian 1967: 29)
Give a woman an inch, and she'll start to diet. (Safian 1967: 29)
Give him a dekameter and he'll take a decimeter. (Colombo
1975: 127)
Give him an inch, and he thinks he's a ruler. (Barbour 1963:
100)
Give him an inch and he'll take a mile. (Barbour 1964: 295)
Give some weeds an inch and they'll take a yard! (McLellan
1996: 18)
Give them [bugs] an inch, and they'll take the whole yard.
(Amdro insecticide advertisement). (*Parade Magazine*, March
20, 1994: 17)

Give Them an Inch, and They'll Take the Whole Yard.

Win the war against fire ants at your house with AMDRO.

There's only one sure way to control fire ants. Kill the queen of the mound. Only AMDRO® fire ant insecticide is *specially formulated* to kill the queen. And when the queen dies, the whole mound dies.

Fire ants think of AMDRO as delicious food. The worker ants eat the bait and take it to the queen, deep inside the mound. The queen eats the bait and dies. So does the colony, usually in less than a week.

AMDRO is clean, odorless, and easy to use. Simply apply twice a year throughout your yard using a hand-held spreader, or treat mounds individually. A little goes a long way, too. The average size lawn can be broadcast with just 3/4 cup of AMDRO. So it's very economical to use.

Remember, left untreated, fire ants can take over your whole yard. Don't take chances. Protect your family with AMDRO.

AMERICA'S #1 FIRE ANT KILLER.

KILLS THE QUEEN.

Always read and follow label directions.

When I lay with my bouncing Nell,
I gave her an inch, and she took an ell:
But I think in this case it was damnable hard,
When I gave her an inch, she'd want more than a yard. (Reisner
1971: 129)

Give the devil his due.
(DAP 146; ODEP 304; CODP 106; MPPS 166; NTC 93)
{Even bad people can do good deeds which should be recognized
and appreciated.}
Give the devil his due, but be sure there isn't much due him.
(Safian 1967: 13)
Give the devil his pew. (Farman 1989)
Give the egotist his due: he never goes around talking about
other people. (Esar 1968: 260)
Give the psychoanalist his due: he is the only one who can make
a domineering person take it lying down. (Esar 1968: 644)
In giving the devil his due, you are liable to give yourself away.
(Ed Howe, in Esar 1968: 217)

God helps those who help themselves.
(DAP 255; ODEP 310; CODP 108; MPPS 259-260; NTC 95)
{You must make the effort yourself if you want to succeed.}
A thief is another man who believes that heaven helps those who
help themselves. (Esar 1968: 807)
God help those who do not help themselves. (Safian 1967: 40;
Wilson Mizner, in Berman 1997: 162)
God helps those that get caught helping themselves. (Anonymous
1965: 289)
God helps those who help themselves, and the government helps
those who don't. (McKenzie 1980: 209)
God helps those who help themselves... murmured the thief as
he broke a window and helped himself to a TV set. (Sydney J.
Harris, in Berman 1997: 162)
God never helps those who are caught helping themselves. (DAP
255)

Heaven help those who help others to help themselves. (Esar
1968: 380)
If God helped those who help themselves, those who help
themselves wouldn't have to hire expensive lawyers. (Leo
Rosten, in Berman 1997: 162)
"It is in vain to help those who don't help themselves," as the
chap said in the apple-tree. (Mieder and Kingsbury 1994: 61)
Lawyers help those who help themselves. (Esar 1968: 465)
Obesity is a condition which proves that the Lord does not help
those who help themselves and help themselves and help
themselves. (Julian Brown, in Berman 1997: 162)

Good fences make good neighbors.
(DAP 206; CODP 112; MPPS 219; NTC 95-96)
{It is good to keep some distance and privacy among neighbors.}
Good fences make good neighbors...more comfortable while they
gossip. (Berman 1997: 134)
Good pitbulls make good neighbors. (Liu and Vasselli 1996)
The fence that makes good neigbors needs a gate to make good
friends. (Jacob M. Braude, Berman 1997: 135)

Great minds run in the same channel.
[Great minds think alike].
(DAP 411; ODEP 326; CODP 116; MPPS 412; NTC 97)
{Clever people think in the same way.}
Great minds drink alike. (Williams & Humbert sherry advertise-
ment). (*Punch*, August 28, 1963: x; and November 6, 1963:
xxii)
Great minds run in the same channel and others in the same
gutter. (Barbour 1964: 296)
Two minds seldom run in the same channels - at least, not where
there's only one television set at home. (Esar 1968: 801)

Great [Mighty] oaks from little acorns grow.
(DAP 435; ODEP 584; CODP 116; MPPS 458; NTC 97)
{The most impressive things or people have humble origins.}

Alcohol can now be produced from acorns, and the song will soon be: "Tall larks from little acorns grow." (Loomis 1949: 356)
Great aches from little corns grow. (Loomis 1949: 356)
Great aches from little toe corns grow. (Safian 1967: 41)
Mighty oafs from little acorns grow. (George Lichty, in Berman 1997: 309)

Half a loaf is better than no bread [none].
(DAP 382; ODEP 344; CODP 118; MPPS 280; NTC 98)
{A part of something, something small and not precious is better than nothing.}
„Half a leaf is better than none," as Eve said to Adam. (Esar 1968: 467)
Half a loaf is better than a whole one if there is much else. (Bierce 1958: 120; Barbour 1963: 100)
Half a loaf is better than no time off. (Prochnow 1988: 426)
Half a loaf is better than none...but keep your hands off of my half. (Berman 1997: 238)
Half a loaf is better than not going to college at all. (Esar 1968: 153)
Half a loafer is better than no husband at all. (Safian 1967: 43)
Half a love is better than none. (Safian 1967: 44)
If you can't get half a loaf, take a whole one - a whole loaf is better than no bread. (Josh Billings, in Berman 1997: 239)

Half the world [One half of the world] does not know how the other half lives.
(DAP 677; ODEP 344; CODP 119; MPPS 280; NTC 98-99)
{People don't know much about the fate of others.}
"Ah, Mrs. Mudge, one half of the world is ignorant of how the other half lives."
"Not in this village, Miss." (Copeland 1965: 195)
Another case where one half doesn't know how the other half lives is the man with a split personality. (Esar 1968: 760)
Half the world doesn't know how his better half lives. (Esar

92

1968: 867)
Half the world doesn't know how many things the other half is
paying installments on. (Safian 1967: 37)
Half the world doesn't know how the other half lives, but is
always trying to find out. (Esar 1968: 200)
Half the world doesn't know how the other half lives, but it has
its suspicions. (Esar 1968: 787)
Half the world doesn't know how the other half lives - but it
isn't the fault of the confession magazines or the gossip columns.
(Safian 1967: 15)
Half the world doesn't know how the other half lives, but not in
a small town. (Esar 1968: 744)
Half the world doesn't know how the other half lives - but
they're sure trying to find out. (Safian 1967: 15)
Half the world doesn't know how the other half lives
If it did, it wouldn't pay its bills either. (Safian 1967: 22)
Half the world knows how the other half ought to live. (Esar
1968: 249)
If half the world doesn't know how the other half lives, it's not
the fault of the confession magazines. (Esar 1952: 202; Proch-
now 1988: 435)
If half the world knew how the other half lives, they wouldn't
pay their bills either. (Esar 1968: 77)
What every wife wants to know: how the other half lives.
(Copeland 1965: 788)

Handsome is as handsome does.
(DAP 278; ODEP 348; CODP 121; MPPS 286; NTC 99)
{Deeds and not good looks show that someone is a good
person.}
A badly cross-eyed Philadelphia woman is said to be really
beautiful when she is asleep. A case of handsome is when
handsome dozes. (Loomis 1949: 355)
Crazy is as crazy does. (*Time*, February 2, 1998: 66)
Handsome is as handsome does - is the motto of all unattractive
people. (Esar 1968: 831)

Handsome is as the photographer does. (Anonymous 1908: 23)
Handsome is what makeup does. (Berman 1977: 177)
India is as Indira does. (*New York Times Magazine*, April 4, 1976: 19)
IQ is as IQ does. (Feibleman 1978: 20)

Hard work never hurt [killed] anybody.
(DAP 675; ODEP 917; MPPS 702)
{Serious work does not harm anybody.}
Hard work never hurt anybody
But lots of folks wear themselves out running away from it. (Safian 1967: 25)
Hard work never hurt anyone who hired someone else to do it. (Esar 1968: 884)
Hard work never killed anybody...but who wants to be its first victim? (Berman 1997: 456)
Hard work never killed anybody, but why take a chance on being its first victim? (Esar 1968: 844)
Hard work never killed anybody...but you never heard of anyone relaxing to death either. (*Wall Street Journal*, in Berman 1997: 456)
If you think hard work never hurt anybody, you've never paid for any. (McKenzie 1980: 567)
"My old Pappy used to say, 'Son, hard work never hurt anyone - who didn't do it'." (Mingo and Javna 1989: 245)

Haste makes waste.
(DAP 284; ODEP 356; CODP 124; MPPS 289; NTC 100)
{Hurrying will actually slow things down.}
Chaste makes waste. (Reisner 1971: 181; Kandel 1976; Kilroy 1985: 265)
Haste makes less waste. (Xerox advertisement). (*New Yorker*, May 19, 1980: 23)
Haste makes waste - and dented fenders. (Esar 1968: 370)
Haste makes waste; waste makes want; want makes a poor boy a beggar. (DAP 284)

"HASTE MAKES LESS WASTE."

Stephen Winn, President
Fast-Tax (Computer Language Research, Inc.)
Dallas, Texas

Stephen Winn heads one of the most aptly named organizations in America.

Fast-Tax is a computer company that processes taxes. Fast.

Hundreds of thousands of income tax returns are sent here from prominent accounting firms all over the world. And Fast-Tax processes them at speeds of up to a million pages a day.

What's amazing about Fast-Tax isn't that it's so efficient or so fast — but rather that it's both at the same time.

How do they do it? With the help of over 1100 hard-working employees, computers, and Xerox 9700 electronic printing systems.

All incoming tax information is fed into a computer. The Xerox system takes this information and, using laser beams, does the staggering job of accurately printing all the returns.

It not only selects and prints the proper forms, but actually fills them out at the same time. It makes the necessary number of sets, and even collates them automatically. All this in a fraction of the time, space, and effort it would take otherwise.

Which enables Fast-Tax to manage information the way it should be managed.

With a minimum of waste. And a maximum of haste.

XEROX

Haste makes waste; waste makes want; want makes strife between a good man and his wife. (DAP 284)
Haste makes gettin' where you're going sooner. (*The Burlington Free Press*, June 5, 1992: without pages)
Make haste, not waste. (Toyota advertisement). (*New Yorker*, july 23, 1979: 42; *Newsweek*, July 23, 1979: 35)
Taste makes waist. (Safian 1967: 41)
Too much taste makes waist. (Esar 1968: 794)

He who dances must pay the fiddler [the piper].
(DAP 133; ODEP 615; CODP 57; MPPS 495; NTC 169)
{1. If you want to do something, you have to pay the cost of an enterprise. 2. You have to accept the consequences of your actions.}
He who dances must pay the fiddler - also the florist, the doorman, the parking lot attendant, the headwaiter, the hat-check girl, and the baby-sitter. (Safian 1967: 15)
He who dances must pay the piper - also the waiter and the hat-check girl. (Esar 1968: 202)
He who dances must pay the piper... and he who pipes must pay the plumber. (Berman 1997: 75)

He who fights and runs away may live to fight another day.
(DAP 207; ODEP 256; CODP 93; MPPS 222; NTC 106)
{Running away from an uneven fight will give you a better chance of surviving and continuing your fight later on.}
"He who chickens out and runs away will chicken out another day." (Mingo and Javna 1989: 45)
He who courts and does not wed may have to come to court instead. (Esar 1952: 252)
He who courts and runs away lives to court another day. (Henny Youngman, in Berman 1997: 135)
He who drinks one glass a day,
Will live to die some other way. (Fuller 1943: 95)
He who fights and runs away, lives. (Esar 1968: 306)
"He who fights and runs away lives to run away another day."

(Mingo and Javna 1989: 212)

He who loves and runs away may live to love another day. (Esar 1968: 594)

He who stops to look each way lives to cross the street another day. (Berman 1997: 135)

He who stops to look each way will live to drive another day. (Safian 1967: 37; Esar 1968: 246)

He who hesitates is lost.

(DAP 299; ODEP 909; CODP 127; MPPS 306; NTC 106)

{In order to achieve your goal, you have to act decisively.}

He who hesitates had better have a good alibi when he gets home. (Safian 1967: 29)

He who hesitates is bossed. (Barbour 1963: 100; Safian 1967: 29)

He who hesitates is constipated. (Kandel 1976)

He who hesitates is cost-conscious nowadays. (Safian 1967: 29)

He who hesitates is lost – and so is his parking place. (Esar 1968: 383)

He who hesitates is lost, but she who hesitates is won. (Esar 1968: 383)

He who hesitates is lost - but the woman who hesitates is won. (Safian 1967: 18)

He who hesitates is lost - except a bachelor. (Safian 1967: 18; Herbert V. Prochnow, Sr., in Prochnow 1988: 269)

He who hesitates is positively not a tax or installment collector. (Safian 1967: 29)

He who hesitates is probably torn between vice and versa. (Esar 1952: 202)

He who hesitates loses the place to park his car. (Safian 1967: 29)

He who hesitates starts the horns tooting. (Safian 1967: 29)

She who hesitates is lost. (Safian 1967: 29)

Sign in a public dance hall: "He who hesitates is not dancing." (Loomis 1949: 355)

He who laughs last laughs best [longest].
(DAP 361; ODEP 445; CODP 145-146; MPPS 362; NTC 106-107)
{Don't count on success well in advance, it may turn to disappointment.}
He laughs best who laughs least. (Bierce 1958: 120)
He who laughs first laughs loudest. (DAP 361)
He who laughs last at the boss's jokes probably isn't very far from retirement. (McKenzie 1980: 52)
He who laughs last didn't get the point anyway. (DAP 361)
He who laughs last doesn't get the joke. (Kandel 1976)
He who laughs last is generally an Englishman. (Loomis 1949: 355)
He who laughs last is thick headed. (Loomis 1949: 355)
He who laughs last is trying to think of a dirty meaning. (Loomis 1949: 355)
He who laughs last is usually the dumbest. (McKenzie 1980: 292)
He who laughs last, lasts. (Rosten 1972: 28)
He who laughs last, laughs best, but soon gets a reputation for being slow-witted. (Safian 1967: 64)
He who laughs last probably got a different meaning. (Anonymous 1965: 290)
He who laughs last probably has an insecure upper plate. (McKenzie 1980: 292)
He who laughs last, was just the last one to get it. (Liu and Vasselli 1996)
He who laughs, lasts. (McLellan 1996: 133)

Hell hath [has] no fury like a woman scorned.
(DAP 296; CODP 126; MPPS 302; NTC 108)
{No one is angrier than a woman who has been rejected in love or offended.}
Hell has no fury as a woman unadorned. (Safian 1967: 42)
Hell has no fury like a bureaucracy scorned. (Milton Friedman, in Berman 1997: 34)

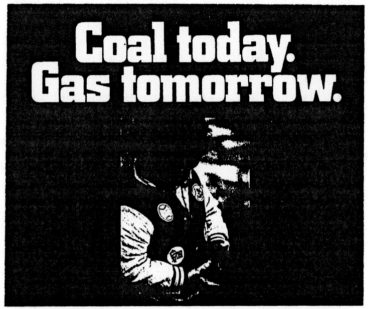

Coal today. Gas tomorrow.

It's one of many ways we're working to get more gas for the 21st century.

Coal is one of America's most plentiful resources. It's been estimated our country has enough to meet our needs for the next three hundred years.

And now it is possible to change this abundant coal into clean gas energy. Not the old-fashioned coal gas of years ago, but an almost exact copy of natural gas. Extremely clean. Extremely efficient because it has the same high energy content.

Gas is the cleanest, most efficient way to use America's coal.

There are other ways coal can be used, of course. It can be burned directly, but this causes pollution problems. It can be used to make electricity, too—but converting it to gas is less costly and more efficient. Turning coal into gas provides at least 25% more useful energy,

at about half the capital investment.

The gas industry and government are working together on many coal gasification research projects. Gas made from coal is one way we can help meet our country's future energy needs.

Getting more gas can't wait any longer.

The gas industry has a long list of other supply projects—like ocean drilling, Arctic drilling, and importing liquefied natural gas.

But much of this work waits on the tough energy decisions America must make—on pricing, offshore drilling leases, new financing alternatives. Meanwhile, it will help if we all conserve gas in our homes and businesses.

Conserve gas. AGA American Gas Association

Hell hath no fury like a well-known overweight comedienne on a liquid diet. (Liu and Vasselli 1996)
Hell hath no fury like a woman at a bargain counter. (Esar 1968: 64)
Hell hath no fury like a woman driver. (Esar 1968: 881)
Hell hath no fury like a woman shorn. (Farman 1989)
Hell hath no fury like a woman who has waited an hour for her husband on the wrong corner. (Esar 1968: 32)
Hell hath no fury like a woman's corn. (Franklin P. Adams, in Esar 1968: 181)
Hell hath no fury like the diary of a woman scorned. (Esar 1968: 218)

Here today, (and) gone tomorrow.
(DAP 299; ODEP 370; MPPS 633; NTC 108-109)
{What or who is available now may soon be gone.}
Bore: a guy who is here today and here tomorrow. (Braude 1955: 42)
Coal today. Gas tomorrow. (American Gas Association advertisement). (*Time*, August 8, 1977: 19)
Hair today, gone tomorrow. (Safian 1967: 42)
Hear today, gone tomorrow. (Audio Den advertisement). (*The Burlington Free Press*, March 25, 1977: 4B)
Here to play, screw tomorrow. (Liu and Vasselli 1996)
In women's hosiery, what's sheer today is gone tomorrow. (Esar 1968: 396)
Women's hosiery
Sheer today, gone tomorrow. (Safian 1967: 50)
You can never tell about husbands: they are here today, gone tomorrow, but where are they tonight? (Esar 1968: 2)

History repeats itself.
(DAP 302; ODEP 374; CODP 128; MPPS 308-309; NTC 109)
{The same kinds of events are liable to happen again.}
A lot of history isn't fit to repeat itself. (McKenzie 1980: 237)
A woman with a past attracts men who hope history will repeat

itself. (Adams 1969: 391)

History does repeat itself, but not as often as old movies. (McKenzie 1980: 237)

History doesn't repeat itself as often as gossip does. (Esar 1968: 674)

History repeats itself, historians repeat one another. (Esar 1968: 386)

It is only national history that "repeats itself." Your private history is repeated by the neighbors. (Edmund and Williams 1921: 215)

We are told that history always repeats itself. But, then, so does television. (McKenzie 1980: 237)

Hitch your wagon to a star.
(DAP 637; ODEP 375; MPPS 661; NTC 109-110)
{You should always set high goals in everything you are doing.}
A press agent is a man who hitches his braggin' to a star. (Berman 1997: 385)

Hitch your wagon to a star, keep your seat, and there you are. (Barbour 1964: 298)

Men who dream of hitching their wagon to a star would be better off to hitch up their pants and go to work. (McKenzie 1980: 141)

Space travel originally started with hitching your wagon to a star. (Esar 1968: 754)

Success is the ability to hitch your wagon to a star while keeping your feet on the ground. (McKenzie 1980: 141)

Home is where the heart is.
(DAP 304; CODP 128; MPPS 313; NTC 110)
{People's home is whatever place they long to be.}
Home is where a fellow should hang his hat, not his head. (McKenzie 1980: 239)

Home is where the asshole is. (Nierenberg 1994: 550)

Home is where the car isn't. (Safian 1967: 36)

"Home is where the computer is." (Mingo and Javna 1989: 100)

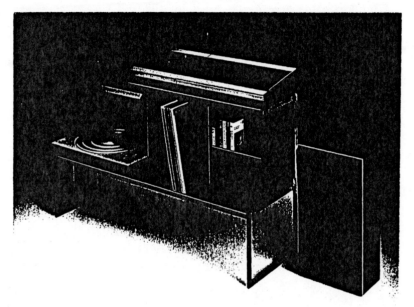

Home is where your hi-fi is.

Bang & Olufsen demonstrates a deeper understanding of domestic harmony.

As well as enjoying the audible pleasures of your hi-fi system, you are going to have to look at it every day for years. Use it. Dust it. Live with it. And unless the system is in sympathy with the rest of your furnishings, it's going to start looking and feeling uncomfortably like a sore thumb in less than a fortnight.

You wouldn't put your sideboard in the garden shed, so why keep a rack full of hardware in your lounge? There is an alternative technology – a better way of giving hi-fi units house-room. The Bang & Olufsen way.

One of our contributions to economic home improvement is the Beosystem 1700C, with its own made-to-measure double decker cabinet. For around £599* you get wall-to-wall music from radio, records and cassette tapes. The 2 x 30 watts receiver covers Long, Medium and FM wavebands, with 5 pre-set stations for instant tuning.

The automatic record deck has an ultra-low mass arm and pickup for optimum tracking with minimal record wear. The Doibyised cassette deck handles ferric, chrome and metal tapes and is very easy to use despite its many advanced features. Beovox S 30 loudspeakers reproduce the music without colouration. And the black lacquered cabinet accommodates everything beautifully – including your favourite records and tapes, disc cleaners, headphones and other hi-fi accessories.

The complete system as illustrated costs rather less than you would pay if buying the units individually (which you can, of course, and build up your system piece by piece as the family budget allows).

Test the Beosystem 1700C for quality and value at your nearest Bang & Olufsen dealer (he's listed in Yellow Pages) or write for further details to Bang & Olufsen UK Limited, Dept A, Eastbrook Road, Gloucester GL4 7DE. Telephone (0452) 21591.

*Typical selling price excluding records and cassettes.

Bang&Olufsen

Home is where the house is. (Weller 1982)
Home is where the Howard is. (Howard Bank advertisement).
(*The Burlington Free Press*, April 28, 1985: 9F)
Home is where the mortgage is. (Wurdz 1904; Anonymous
1908: 72; DAP 304)
Home is where you hang your head. (Kilroy 1985: 176)
Home is where your hi-fi is. (Bang & Olufsen hi-fi adver-
tisement). (*Punch*, February 18, 1981: inside back cover; and
November 11, 1981: inside back cover)
Home is where your Bus is. (Volkswagen advertisement). (*Better
Homes & Gardens*, August 1978: 5)

Honesty is the best policy.
(DAP 305; ODEP 380; CODP 129; MPPS 314; NTC 111)
{Honesty will pay in the long run.}
Honesty is also the best foreign policy. (McKenzie 1980: 217)
Honesty is one business policy that will never have to be
changed to keep up with the times. (McKenzie 1980: 58)
Honesty is the best policy, because good lawyers come high.
(Esar 1968: 465)
Honesty is the best policy..."but," as a politician said, "there
comes a time to put principle aside and do what's right."
(Berman 1997: 193)
Honesty is the best policy, but life insurance is even better for
the widow. (Esar 1968: 478)
Honesty is the best policy...but not the cheapest. (Mark Twain,
in Berman 1997: 192)
Honesty is the best policy, but there are too few policy holders.
(Esar 1968: 230)
"Honesty is the best policy." O.K.! Now, what's the *second*-best
policy? (*New Yorker*, May 15, 1978: 38)
Honesty is the best policy only when dishonesty does not work
to your advantage. (Liu and Vasselli 1996)
Honesty is the best policy; there's less competition. (Safian
1967: 12)
Honesty is the best policy, though it may not pay the largest

dividents. (DAP 305)
Honesty is the best policy, unless of course you are an exceptionally good liar. (Esar 1968: 472)
Honesty is the best policy - when there is money in it. (Mark Twain, in Esar 1968: 392)
Honesty is the bust policy. (Safian 1967: 41)
Honesty may be the best policy, but falsies prove it is not always the best policy. (Esar 1968: 105)
Honesty may be the best policy, but life insurance is more satisfactory to the widow. (McKenzie 1980: 306)
Incumbency is the best policy. (*Time*, November 5, 1979: 28)

Hope springs eternal (in the human breast).
(DAP 309; CODP 130; NTC 112)
{Hope is part of human life.}
Baseball springs eternal. (*Time*, April 26, 1976: cover page)
Hope springs eternal in the human breast, but it often summers elsewhere. (Esar 1968: 394)
Hope springs eternal in the human breast - that's why a new restaurant is crowded. (Esar 1968: 679)
Hope springs eternal in the human heart, but with some the spring is getting very weak. (McKenzie 1980: 232)
Hope springs eternal - in the suburban gardener. (Safian 1967: 16)

If a thing [a job] is worth doing, it is worth doing well.
[Anything worth doing is worth doing well].
(DAP 339; ODEP 921; CODP 252; MPPS 619; NTC 114)
{If you are going to do something, do it to the best of your ability.}
Anything worth doing has probably already been done by someone else. (Berman 1997: 12)
Anything worth doing is worth hiring someone who knows how to do it right. (Berman 1997: 12)
If a thing's worth doing, it's worth doing late. (Frederick Oliver, in Flavell 1993: 148)

TIME

BASEBALL SPRINGS ETERNAL

Make sure that what you are doing well is worth doing. (Feibleman 1978: 95)
What is worth doing is worth the trouble of asking somebody to
do it. (Bierce 1958: 120)

If at first you don't succeed, try, try again.
(DAP 570; CODP 244; MPPS 604; NTC 114)
{Keep trying until you finally succeed.}
If at first you didn't try Pabst - try again! (Pabst beer advertise-
ment). (*Fortune*, May 1936: 203)
If at first you're not believed, lie, lie again. (Esar 1968: 474)
If at first you're not relieved, try a little bran. (Liu and Vasselli
1996)
If at first you do succeed, it's probably your father's business.
(Esar 1968: 303)
If at first you do succeed, try something harder. (Prochnow
1988: 411)
If at first you do succeed, try to hide your astonishment.
(Berman 1997: 392)
If at first you don't recede, diet, diet again. (Anonymous 1961:
200)
If at first you don't succeed, blame it on your wife. (Esar 1968:
292)
If at first you don't succeed, blame somebody. (Berman 1997:
391)
If at first you don't succeed - cheat! (Kilroy 1985: 18)
If at first you don't succeed, cry, cry again. (Esar 1968: 863; *St.
Louis Post-Dispatch*, January 31, 1975: 12D)
If at first you don't succeed, date the boss's daughter. (Esar
1968: 204)
If at first you don't succeed, don't be an idiot, quit! (Anonymous
1965: 290)
If at first you don't succeed, find out why before you try again.
(McKenzie 1980: 481)
If at first you don't succeed - forget it. (Esar 1968: 291)
If at first you don't succeed, give up. (Anonymous 1961: 200)

"'Honesty is the best policy.' O.K.! Now, what's the *second*-best policy?"

. .

"We do things a little differently around here, Haskell. If at
first you don't succeed, you're fired."

If at first you don't succeed, have a beer. (*New Yorker*, April 8, 1991: 63)

If at first you don't succeed, it's probably not your father's business. (Safian 1967: 35)

If at first you don't succeed, just keep suckin' till you do suck seed. (Anonymous 1961: 200)

If at first you don't succeed, keep on sucking till you do succeed. (DAP 570)

If at first you don't succeed, pry, pry again. (Esar 1968: 200)

If at first you don't succeed, slide for second. (Loomis 1949: 357)

If at first you don't succeed, subcontract it out. (*New Yorker*, April 13, 1998: 56)

If at first you don't succeed -
suck, suck again
change your major
get rid of your ego and it won't matter
try cocaine - right on - all around my brain... (Nierenberg 1994: 549-550)

If at first you don't succeed, try a little ardor. (Safian 1967: 47; McLellan 1996: 13)

If at first you don't succeed, try doing it the way your wife told you. (Esar 1968: 10; McKenzie 1980: 483)

If at first you don't succeed, try for second. (Anonymous 1961: 200)

If at first you don't succeed, try looking in the wastebasket for the directions. (McKenzie 1980: 483)

If at first you don't succeed, try playing second base. (Esar 1968: 65)

If at first you don't succeed, try reading the directions. (McLellan 1996: 54)

If at first you don't succeed, try reading the instructions. (Metcalf 1993: 205)

If at first you don't succeed, try something else. (Mingo and Javna 1989: 213)

If at first you don't succeed, try, try, a gun. (Anonymous 1965:

108

290)
If at first you don't succeed, try, try again; then quit - there's no use being pigheaded. (Safian 1967: 14)
If at first you don't succeed, try, try again. Then quit. There's no use making a fool of yourself. (W. C. Fields, in Woods 1967: 31)
If at first you don't succeed, try, try again - to get somebody else to do it. (McKenzie 1980: 480)
If at first you don't succeed, try trying. (McKenzie 1980: 394)
If at first you don't succeed with a girl, try a little ardor. (Loomis 1949: 357)
If at first you don't succeed, you are fired. (*St. Louis Post-Dispatch*, January 31, 1975: 12D; *New Yorker*, April 17, 1978: 34)
If at first you don't succeed, you're average. (Kehl 1977: 290)
If at first you don't succeed, you're like most other people. (Herbert V. Prochnow, Sr., in Prochnow 1988: 270)
If at first you don't succeed, you're running about average. (McKenzie 1980: 481)
If at first you don't succeed, you'll get a lot of unsolicited advice. (McKenzie 1980: 482)
If at first you don't succeed, your relatives will tell one another just why you'll never succeed. (Esar 1968: 669)
If at first you succeed, try again. (Galleria Plaza Hotel [Houston] advertisement). (*Sky*, November 1977: 74-75)

If the shoe [cap] fits, wear it.
(DAP 82, 536; ODEP 101; CODP 36, 227-228; MPPS 91, 560; NTC 116)
{If the words of blame or criticism apply to you, you should accept them.}
If the cap fits, wear it!
Does Andy wear his cap in bed? No, Florie is on the pill. (Kilroy 1985: 408)
If the dress no longer fits, peel it. (Dole bananas advertisement). (*Woman's Day*, May 1975: 57)

If the dress no longer fits, peel it.

Find yourself in and out of tight squeezes?
Then make that next snack a delicious Dole banana.

It may come as a surprise to you, but a medium-size Dole banana has only about 85 calories. Which makes it filling, but not fattening.

Maybe you can tell your friends the dress shrunk in the wash. But by all means, start peeling!

The Dole Banana. As a snack, it's a natural.

110

If the shoe fits it probably isn't the one the army issued you.
(*The Burlington Free Press*, November 19, 1975: 27)
If the shoe fits, it's out of style. (Safian 1967: 40)
If the sneaker is endorsed by a professional basketball player,
wear it. (Liu and Vasselli 1996)
Like I always say, If the seat fits, wear it.
Children should be seated, not hurt. (Child Passenger Law
advertisement). (*Chicago*, June 1983: 290A)

If you're angry [When angry] count to ten.
(DAP 19-20; ODEP 14; MPPS 615)
{Ty to control your anger.}
Before you get angry at someone's faults, always count ten – ten
of your own. (Esar 1968: 184)
When angry, count to ten, and when very angry - swear. (Safian
1967: 16)
When angry count to ten before speaking. When very angry
count to one hundred and then don't speak. (McKenzie 1980: 23)

If you want a thing done well [well done], do it yourself.
(DAP 155; ODEP 865; CODP 270-271; MPPS 619; NTC 119)
{Don't rely on other people, you are the best person to do things
properly for yourself.}
If you want a thing to be well done, don't do it yourself - hire
a specialist. (Esar 1968: 101)
If you want a thing well done, let it cook. (Berman 1997: 105)
If you want work well done, select a busy man - the other kind
has no time. (Hubbard 1973: 103)

Ignorance is bliss.
(DAP 325; CODP 135; MPPS 335; NTC 231)
{Sometimes it seems good not to know everything.}
If ignorance is bliss, he must be Mr. Happy! (Metcalf 1993:
121)
"If ignorance is bliss, this is Eden." (Diane Chambers, in Mingo
and Javna 1989: 225)

Children should be seated, not hurt.

On July 1, Illinois' new Child Passenger Restraint Law
goes into effect. It requires all children under 2 years old
to be in a car seat whenever they travel.
We think it's a good law and want to make it work for everyone.
Find out how you can help
by listening to Wally Phillips, weekday mornings.

720 AM WGN Radio is Chicago.

If ignorance is bliss, why aren't more people happy? (McLellan 1996: 238; Berman 1997: 200)

If ignorance was bliss, we'd all be a whole lot happier. (McKenzie 1980: 229)

Ignorance is bliss, but not when you're a dropout. (Esar 1968: 410)

Ignorance is bliss only when you have more money than you know what to do with. (Esar 1968: 857)

Ignorance is blister when one is suntanned. (Safian 1967: 45)

Ignorance is not bliss - it's oblivion. (Philip Wylie, in Berman 1997: 200)

Ignorance must not be bliss or lots of people would be jumping for joy all the time. (McKenzie 1980: 261)

Just as soon as we discover that ignorance is bliss, it isn't. (Esar 1968: 410)

Ignorance of the law is no excuse.
(DAP 325; ODEP 396; CODP 135; MPPS 335; NTC 120)
{People who don't know that something is against the law can still be punished for doing it.}

Don't forget the fact that ignorance of the law is what keeps our higher courts functioning. (McKenzie 1980: 293)

Ignorance of the law does not prevent the losing lawyer from collecting his bill. (Copeland 1965: 782)

Ignorance of the law excuses no man - from practicing it. (Addison Mizner, in Woods 1967: 158)

Ignorance of the law excuses no man who retains poor counsel. (Woods 1967: 158)

Ignorance of the law is no excuse, but it's better than no alibi at all. (McKenzie 1980: 16)

Ignorance of the law is no excuse, unless you can afford to hire a good lawyer. (Esar 1968: 463)

Ignorance of the law prevents a lawyer from winning your case, but not from collecting his fee. (Esar 1968: 464)

Lawyer: the only man in whom ignorance of the law is not punished. (Elbert Hubbard, in Braude 1955: 214)

In union there is strength.
[Union is strength].
(DAP 625; ODEP 854; CODP 266; MPPS 656; NTC 224)
{People working together have more power.}
In union there is strength, and in unions even more strength.
(Esar 1968: 457)
"In union there is strength," as the landlady said when she mixed
lard with butter for her boarders. (Mieder and Kingsbury 1994:
144)
"Union is not always strength," as the sailor said when he saw
the purser mixing his rum with water. (Mieder and Kingsbury
1994: 144)

It is better [more blessed] to give than to receive.
(DAP 252; ODEP 53; CODP 20; MPPS 253; NTC 122)
{Being generous is better than being in need or on the receiving
end.}
Buy two: It's better to give *and* receive. (Cutty Sark Whiskey
advertisement). (*Time*, December 6, 1976: 49)
If it is more blessed to give than to receive, then most of us are
content to let the other fellow have the greater blessing. (Shailer
Mathews, in Berman 1997: 159)
It is better to give and to receive. (Adler typewriter advertise-
ment). (*New York Times Magazine*, December 4, 1977: 130)
If it is more blessed to give than to receive, why are we content
to let others get all the blessings? (Esar 1968: 82)
It is more blessed to give and then receive. (Berman 1997: 159)
It is more blessed to give than to receive... advice. (Berman
1997: 159)
"It is more blessed to give than to receive," as the school boy
said ven the master flogged him. (Mieder and Kingsbury 1994:
52)
It is more blessed to give than to receive... but it can be more
expensive. (Berman 1997: 159)
It is more blessed to give than to receive - but lots of folks
prefer others to have the blessing. (Safian 1967: 18)

It is more blessed to give than to receive - if you are a judge handing out a sentence. (Safian 1967: 18)
It may be more blessed to give than to receive, but it sure costs more. (McKenzie 1980: 205)
Philanthropy is based on the principle that it's better to give than to receive - as long as it's tax deductible. (Esar 1968: 595)
Sometimes it's better to receive. (Haviland China advertisement). (*New York Times Magazine*, December 4, 1977: 22; *Esquire*, November 1979: 15 [St. John's Bay Rum advertisement])
When making out your income tax, remember that it's better to give than to deceive. (Esar 1968: 419)
Why Edwin Newman believes it is better to give than to gift. (American Heritage Dictionary advertisement). (*Time*, November 28, 1977: 129; and December 5, 1977: 88)

It never rains but it pours.
[When it rains, it pours].
(DAP 498; ODEP 663; CODP 212; MPPS 523; NTC 124-125)
{Events, especially misfortunes, always occur in large numbers all at once.}
At the Aruba Beach Club
if it rains,
we pour! (Aruba Beach Club advertisement). (*New York Times Magazine*, June 3, 1979: 42)
It never just pours.
It reigns.
Waterford. (Waterford crystal advertisement). (*New Yorker*, April 9, 1979: 51; *Bon Appetit*, June 1979: 3)
Villa Banfi: When it pours, it reigns. (Villa Banfi wines advertisement). (*Ski*, October 1976: 44; *Time*, August 29, 1977: 7)
When it pours, it reigns. (Waterford crystal advertisement). (*New York Times magazine*, October 16, 1977: 3; *New Yorker*, February 6, 1978: front inside cover))
When it rains, we shine...
And when it shines, we shine. (Heritage Plantation Museum advertisement). (*Time*, December 5, 1997: 60)

WHEN IT POURS,
IT REIGNS.

A timely investment in
timeless art.
   Legendary Waterford crystal.
   Born in fire in the ancient
Irish city of Waterford.
   Blown by mouth & cut wholly
by hand, with heart.
   Each masterwork is faintly etched
with the one & only signature that
identifies it as authentic.
   Waterford.
   The world's most desired crystal.
   Man lives not by water alone.

Free stemware booklet, Waterford Crystal, 225 Fifth Avenue, NY 10010.   Photo: Penn

WATERFORD

When it snows, it reigns. (Audi advertisement). (*The Burlington Free Press*, February 8, 1994: 4A)

It's a long lane that has no turning.
(DAP 359; ODEP 480; CODP 155; MPPS 360; NTC 121)
{An existence without change is boring.}
"It is a long lane that has no turning," as the eel said to the aqueduct. (Mieder and Kingsbury 1994: 71)
It's a long road that has no joy-ride. (Loomis 1949: 356)
It's a short road that has no advertising signs. (Safian 1967: 38)
It's a strong stomach that has no turning. (Safian 1967: 40; Oliver Herford, in Prochnow 1988: 141)

It's a wise child that knows its own father.
(DAP 96; ODEP 899; CODP 278; MPPS 111; NTC 121-122)
{A person can never be sure that a certain man is the father.}
It's a wise child that resembles its rich relatives. (Esar 1968: 668)
It's a wise fraternity man that knows his own clothes. (Colorado Dodo, in Prochnow 1988: 405)
It's a wise horse that knows its own fodder. (Esar 1968: 395)
It's a wise horse that noses his own fodder. (Loomis 1949: 354)

It's always darkest just before the dawn.
[The darkest hour is just before the dawn].
(DAP 134; ODEP 168; CODP 57; MPPS 327-328; NTC 197)
{Bad times don't continue forever; sooner or later things will improve.}
It's always dullest just before the yawn. (*Life*, ca. 1925, in Berman 1997: 75)
"Just remember, things are always darkest before they go pitch black." (Kelly Robinson, in Mingo and Javna 1989: 116)
Poker - It's darkest just before you've drawn. (Copeland 1965: 772)

It's an ill wind that blows nobody any good.
(DAP 656; ODEP 401; CODP 136; MPPS 685-686; NTC 126-127)
{In every misfortune, difficulty or loss there is someone who benefits by it.}
It's an ill wind that blows a saxophone. (Safian 1967: 35)
It's an ill wind that blows when you leave the hairdresser. (Phyllis Diller, in Berman 1997: 444)
It's an ill wind that shows no pretty knees. (Copeland 1965: 787)

It's better to have loved and lost than never to have loved at all.
(CODP 20; NTC 219-220)
{You gain so much from experiencing love that you shouldn't avoid it for fear of rejection.}
Bachelors
'Tis better to have loved and lost - indeed, lots better. (Safian 1967: 47)
Better to have failed your Wasserman test than never to have loved at all. (Reisner 1971: 147)
Better to have loved and lost than to have spent your whole damn life with him. (Shaw 1980; Kilroy 1985: 425)
Here's what the old man said
With a grin and a funny drawl -
"Better to have loved a short girl
Than never to have loved a tall." (Rees 1965: 110)
It is better to have loved and lost than to have to do homework for the kids every night. (Safian 1967: 39)
It's better to have kissed amiss than never to have kissed a miss. (Berman 1997: 251)
It's better to have loved and lost - yeah, lots better. (Adams 1959: 150)
My philosophy is that it's better to have loved a short girl than never to have loved at all. (Metcalf 1993: 139)
Occasionally you meet a man who thinks it is better to have loved and married than never to have loved at all. (Esar 1968:

491)
"Please remember, and don't ever forget: It is better not to have
been in love than to never have loved at all." (Dwayne Schnei-
der, in Mingo and Javna 1989: 130)
There are two kinds of disillusioned women: those who have
loved and lost, and those who have loved and married. (Esar
1968: 231)
This week's motto: It is better to have loved and lost than to
have run into the house detective. (Adams 1959: 150)
'Tis better to have failed a Wassermann test than never to have
loved at all. (*New Yorker*, no date, 1977: 206)
'Tis better to have loved and lust, than never to have lust at all.
(Kilroy 1985: 277)
'Tis better to have lived and loved
Than never to have lived at all. (Edmund and Williams 1921:
271)
'Tis better to have loved and lost than to be married and
divorced. (Berman 1997: 251)
'Tis better to have loved and lost than to have loved and
married. (Metcalf 1993: 143)
'Tis better to have loved and lost than never to have lost at all.
(Nicholas Murray Butler, in Prochnow 1988: 47)
'Tis better to have loved and lost than to marry and be bossed.
(Esar 1968: 90)
'Tis better to have loved and lust. (Kandel 1976)
'Tis better to have loved and receive alimony than never to have
loved at all. (Esar 1968: 26)
VD may be a drag, but it's better to have a positive Wasserman
test than never to have made it at all. (Yu and Jang 1975: 70)

It's never too late to learn.
(DAP 366; ODEP 563; CODP 181; MPPS 361; NTC 123)
{No matter how intelligent and experienced, people can always
learn more.}
A woman is never too old to yearn. (Safian 1967: 43)
It's funny how we never get too old to learn some new ways to

be foolish. (McKenzie 1980: 187)
It's never too late to learn – and it's never too early either. (Esar 1968: 468)

It's never too late to mend.
(DAP 409; ODEP 563; CODP 181; MPPS 362; NTC 123-124)
{It is never too late to turn over a new leaf and to try to repair something you have done wrong.}
In Congress, it's never too late to amend. (Esar 1968: 416)
It's never too late to spend. (Wurdz 1904; Safian 1967: 36, 40)

It takes all sorts [kinds] to make the world.
(DAP 347; ODEP 11; CODP 4; MPPS 583; NTC 125)
{The world is made up of various types of people.}
It takes all kinds of people to make a world
But lots of nuisances ought to go somewhere and make their own. (Safian 1967: 24)
It takes all kinds of people to unmake the world. (Esar 1968: 886)
It takes all kinds to make the world, and the world certainly looks it. (Esar 1968: 886)
It takes all sorts to make a world...and we've *got* all sorts. (Berman 1997: 459)

It takes two to make a bargain.
(DAP 37; ODEP 852; CODP 265; MPPS 653; NTC 125)
{Both sides should agree if they want to negotiate successfully.}
If it takes two to make a bargain, it takes two to break it. (DAP 37)
It takes two to make a bargain...and a lawyer to write the contract. (Berman 1997: 21)
It takes two to make a bargain, but only one gets it. (Safian 1967: 14)

It takes two to make a quarrel.
(DAP 493; ODEP 852; CODP 265; MPPS 653; NTC 125-126)

IT TAKES TWO TO DRINK "PERNOD"

Pernod est Paris, Paris est Pernod.

A la Francaise
Pour 2 ozs. Pernod over ice.
Fill with water.

The Oddball
Pour 1½ ozs. Pernod over rocks.
Fill with Orange Juice.

Pernod Sour
1½ ozs. Pernod
1½ ozs. Triple Sec.
Juice of one half lemon.
Shake with ice.
Strain into sour glass.

122

{Quarrelling can't be performed alone, participation of two people is always needed for it.}
It takes two to make a quarrel
And three to make it interesting. (Safian 1967: 24)
It takes two to have a quarrel but only one to start it. (DAP 493)
It takes two to make a quarrel, but one can end it. (DAP 493)
It takes two to quarrel, but one gets the blame. (Mieder 1993: 36)

It takes two to tango.
(CODP 265; NTC 126)
{Some things can be accomplished only together with somebody else.}
It takes one to tango. (*Seven Days*, December 13, 1995: 1)
It takes two to drink "Pernod." (Pernod advertisement). (*Gourmet*, June 1974: 65)
It takes two to "Pernod." (Pernod advertisement). (*New York*, November 11, 1974: 100)
It takes two to tangle. (Kandel 1976; Kilroy 1985: 277)
It takes two to untangle. (*USA Weekend*, November 26, 1993: 16)

It will all come out in the wash.
(DAP 640; ODEP 135; MPPS 664)
{Everything will work itself out.}
It will all come out in the wash...and don't get caught in the wringer. (Berman 1997: 435)
It will all come out in the wash and what won't come out in the wash will come out in the rinse. (Barbour 1964: 298)
"It'll all come out in the wash," as the feller said about the tomato soup. (Mieder and Kingsbury 1994: 147)
It'll all come out in the Laudromat. (*The Burlington Free Press*, June 3, 1995: 1C)

Judge not, that ye be not judged.
(DAP 341; ODEP 415; CODP 139; NTC 129)

{Do not criticize other people, for they will have the right to criticize you in return.}
Judge not, that ye be not judged...at least wait until all the evidence is in. (Berman 1997: 207)
Visit, that ye be not visited. (Don Herold, in Esar 1968: 847)

Know thyself.
(DAP 352; ODEP 435; CODP 143; MPPS 355; NTC 132)
{Try to understand your own strengths and weaknesses.}
Know thyself, and *no* thy selfishness. (Esar 1968: 713)
Know thyself...but don't tell anyone. (H. F. Henrichs, in Berman 1997: 211)
Know thyself, but don't tell thy biographer. (Esar 1968: 78)
Know thyself, but tell no one what thou knowest. (Esar 1968: 713)
Mothers advising daughters
NO thyself. (Safian 1967: 51)
The ascetic says: No thyself. (Berman 1997: 212)
The best advice to a dieter is: *No thyself.* (Esar 1968: 711)

Knowledge is power.
(DAP 354; ODEP 436-437; CODP 143; MPPS 356; NTC 133)
{The more one knows, the stronger the influence one can exercise on others.}
Knowledge is power but, no matter how much you know, you still can't run your electric appliances with it. (Esar 1968: 262)
Knowledge is power, but only if a man knows what facts not to bother about. (Robert Lynd, in Esar 1968: 455)
Knowledge is power, but the unnecessary display of it is weakness. (Esar 1968: 232)
Knowledge is power...if you know it about the right people. (*Cynic*, 1905, in Berman 1997: 213)
Knowledge is power only when it is turned on. (McKenzie 1980: 286)
Knowledge, with the right contacts, is more powerful. (Liu and Vasselli 1996)

Laugh and the world laughs with you; cry [weep] and you cry [weep] alone.
(DAP 361-362; CODP 145; NTC 134)
{When you are happy and cheerful, people will be around sharing your interests and feelings; but when you are gloomy or sad, they will tend to keep away from you.}
Cough and the world coughs with you. Fart and you stand alone.
(Trevor Griffiths, in Berman 1997: 217)
Eat and the world eats with you; wash dishes and you wash alone. (Barbour 1963: 99)
Laugh and the world laughs with you - but only if the joke is good. (Adams 1959: 13)
Laugh and the world laughs with you; cry and the other guy has an even better sob story. (McKenzie 1980: 292)
Laugh and the world laughs with you; cry – and the world laughs harder. (Esar 1968: 461)
Laugh, and the world laughs with you.
Cry, and you wet your face. (Rees 1981: 75)
Laugh, and the world laughs with you - snore, and you sleep alone! (Kilroy 1985: 205)
Laugh and the world will laugh with you; think and you will almost die of loneliness. (McKenzie 1980: 293)
Laugh and the world laughs with you, unless you laugh at your own joke. (Esar 1968: 447)
Laugh and the world laughs with you,
Weep and the laugh's on you. (Edmund and Williams 1921: 259)
Laugh, and the world thinks you're an idiot. (Kandel 1976; Kilroy 1985: 201)
Lie and the world lies with you; tell the truth and the world lies about you. (Esar 1968: 828)
Plant and the world plants with you. Weed and you weed alone.
(Dennis Breeze, in Berman 1997: 217)
Quaff and the world quaffs with you, abstain and you drink alone. (Esar 1968: 3)
Smoke and the world smokes with you; swear off and you smoke alone. (Copeland 1965: 787; Safian 1967: 36)

Spy and the world spies with you; get caught and you're on your own. (G. Brown, in Berman 1997: 217)

The world laughs with the man who laughs; if you do not laugh, the world will laugh at you. (Hubbard 1973: 175)

Let bygones be bygones.
(DAP 78; ODEP 96; MPPS 86; NTC 135)
{We should forget our past offenses and problems and start over again.}

Let bygones be bygones....unless your lawyer thinks you have a good chance of winning a lawsuit. (Liu and Vasselli 1996)

"We agreed to let bygones be bygones," as the rooster said after he had searched vainly half an hour for an eye pecked out in a fight. (Mieder and Kingsbury 1994: 18)

Let sleeping dogs lie.
(DAP 160; ODEP 456; CODP 231-232; MPPS 176-177; NTC 135-136)
{Do not do anything that will instigate trouble.}

Another noted proverb was originated in a dog kennel. Their trainer was teaching them to jump over a high fence when a lady came in. "Those dogs can't jump that fence," she insisted. The man quietly replied, *"Let leaping dogs try."* (Howard 1989: 256)

Let dead dogs sleep. (Berman 1997: 103)

Let sleeping dogmas lie. (Berman 1997: 103)

Let sleeping ducks lie. (Rosten 1972: 30)

Let sleeping gods lie. (Kilroy 1985: 434)

Play safe: let sleeping dogs lie, and let lying dogs sleep. (Esar 1968: 239)

Remember what I always say... "Let sleeping dads lie." (*Washington Post*, June 6, 1996: 16E)

Let [Leave] well enough alone.
(DAP 15; ODEP 453; CODP 148; MPPS 676-677; NTC 135)
{Do not try to improve the situation in which things are going well.}

" 'Tis better to have failed a Wassermann test than never to have loved at all."

A hypochondriac is one who can't leave being well enough alone. (Esar 1968: 405)
All progress is due to those who were not satisfied to let well enough alone. (McKenzie 1980: 7)
Doctors should let the well enough alone. (Esar 1968: 237)
If man believed in leaving well enough alone, where would we be? (Mieder 1993: 69)

Life begins at forty.
(DAP 373; CODP 149; NTC 137)
{Life can still have its good side after reaching mid-age.}
It may be true that life begins at forty, but everything else starts to wear out, fall out, or spread out. (McKenzie 1980: 226)
Life may begin at forty, but so does rheumatism. (McKenzie 1980: 305)
Life not only begins at forty - it begins to show. (McKenzie 1980: 302)

Life is just a bowl of cherries.
(DAP 374; MPPS 371; NTC 137)
{Life is good despite its problems.}
If life were a bowl of cherries, chances are two to one that the pickers would go on strike. (McKenzie 1980: 303)
"Life is just a bowl of kumquats." (Mingo and Javna 1989: 119)
Life is just a bowl of pits. (Rodney Dangerfield, in Berman 1997: 227)
Life is just a bowl of toenails. (Rees 1979: 20)
Life is like a bunch of raisins - raisin' heck, raisin' kids, or raisin' money. (S.S. Biddle, in Berman 1997: 227)

Life is just one damned thing after another.
(DAP 374; MPPS 371)
{Life has its problems.}
Life is just one canned thing after another. (Safian 1967: 43)
Life is one damn thing after another
More precisely, the same damn thing over and over. (Safian

128

1967: 24)
The philosopher asked to define the difference between life and
love, said: "Life is just one fool thing after another. Love is two
fool things after each other." (Woods 1967: 277)
"Wife is just one sham thing after another," thought the husband,
as his spouse placed her teeth, hair, shape, and complexion on
the bureau. (Mieder and Kingsbury 1994: 151)

Life is not a bed of roses.
(DAP 374; MPPS 371)
{Life is not always easy.}
A bigamist is a man for whom life is a bed of ruses. (Esar 1968:
76)
If life were a bed of roses, some people wouldn't be happy until
they developed an allergy. (McKenzie 1980: 303)
Life is a bed of ruses. (Kilroy 1985: 411)
Life is like a bed of roses - full of pricks. (Kilroy 1985: 370)
Marriage is a bed of roses - Look out for the thorns. (Kilroy
1985: 420)
Wolves
Life is a bed of ruses. (Safian 1967: 47)

Life is what you make it.
(DAP 374)
{You are responsible for your own life.}
For a while, life is what you make it, until your children begin
to make it even worse. (Berman 1997: 234)
For most of us, life is what we make it, but for the pedestrian,
it's if he makes it. (Prochnow 1988: 400)
Life is as you take it, and there are many ways of committing
suicide. (Esar 1968: 780)
Life is what we make it - but for the pedestrian, if he makes it.
(Safian 1967: 15)
Life is what you make it, or what it makes you. (McKenzie
1980: 304)
Life is what you make it, until some nuisance comes around and

makes it worse. (Safian 1967: 13)
Life is what you make it until somebody makes it worse. (Mc-
Kenzie 1980: 303)
Out in the country, life is what you make it, but in the city it too
often is what you make. (Prochnow 1988: 416)
The man who believes life is what you make it, usually marries
the woman who believes life is what you make. (Esar 1968: 477)

Lightning never strikes twice (in the same place).
[Lightning never strikes the same place twice].
(DAP 377; CODP 150; MPPS 374; NTC 138)
{The same misfortune or unpredictable thing never occurs twice
in the same way to the same person.}
Lightning never strikes mice. (Margo 1982: 16)
Lightning never strikes twice in the same place except when it
forgets where it struck last. (DAP 377)
Lightning never strikes twice in the same place
It doesn't need to. (Safian 1967: 22)
Lightning never strikes twice in the same place – once is enough.
(Esar 1968: 479)
Teacher was giving a lesson on the wonders and powers of
nature, and in the course of it she questioned, "Now, Tommy,
can you tell us why it is that lightning never strikes twice in the
same place?"
"I'll say," replied Tommy. "It's 'cause after it strikes once the
same place ain't there any more." (Esar 1945: 267)
Lightning never strikes the same place twice...but it's neverthe-
less good practice to steer clear of the locality where it's been in
the habit of hitting. (William C. Hunter, in Berman 1997: 235)

Like father, like son.
(DAP 201; ODEP 248; CODP 90-91; MPPS 216; NTC 139)
{The child often exhibits similar character traits as the father.}
Like mom, like son. (*The Burlington Free Press*, August 20,
1987: 1D)
Like son, like father. (Johnson's baby powder advertisement).

130

(*People*, July 2, 1979: 11)
When it comes to thinning hair, like father, like son doesn't have
to apply. (Nioxin scalp fitness advertisement). (*Playboy*, July
1988: 9)

Live and learn.
(DAP 381; ODEP 473; CODP 153; MPPS 380)
{We always learn something new.}
Live and lean. (Weller 1982)
Live and learn
But by the time you've learned it's too late to live. (Safian 1967:
19)
Live and learn; die and forget all. (DAP 381)

Look before you leap.
(DAP 384; ODEP 482; CODP 156; MPPS 383; NTC 141-142)
{Think carefully what you are going to do before you do it.}
A bachelor is a man who looks before he leaps - and then
doesn't leap. (Metcalf 1993: 195)
A bachelor looks before he leaps, then stays where he is.
(McKenzie 1980: 37)
He who looks before he leaps is less likely to leap. (Feibleman
1978: 121)
"Look before you bite," said the man eating chestnuts. (Loomis
1949: 355)
Look before you leak. (Farman 1989)
Look before you leap, but look ahead, not behind. (Esar 1968:
118)
Look before you leave. (North Carolina Travel advertisement).
(*Glamour*, February 1981: 131; Mieder 1989: 274)
Lovers
Look before you lip. (Safian 1967: 50)

Love is blind.
(DAP 388; ODEP 490; CODP 158; MPPS 386; NTC 142)
{When we are in love, we don't see the faults of the beloved.}

If Love is blind, and God is love, and Ray Charles is blind, then God plays the piano.
No, Ray Charles is God.
Baloney! God is blind. (Yu and Jang 1975: 22)
If love is blind, how can there be love at first sight? (Esar 1968: 491)
If love is blind, maybe that's why you see so many spectacles in the park. (Adams 1959: 150)
It's not easy for a beautiful girl to believe that love is blind. (Esar 1968: 69)
Love is blind, and marriage is an eye opener. (Esar 1968: 491)
Love is blind - and when you get married you get your eyesight back. (Kilroy 1985: 261)
Love is blind, but neighbors aren't. (DAP 388)
Love is blind, but not stone blind when a girl gets a diamond with a flaw in it. (Safian 1967: 13)
Love is blind, but your mother-in-law isn't. (Esar 1952: 220)
Love is blind, deaf, and speechless. (DAP 388)
Love is blind, so is hatred. (DAP 388)
Love is blind
with sex in mind
but
Don't be resigned
It always takes
two of a kind. (Reisner 1971: 149)
Love is said to be blind, but I know lots of fellows in love who can see twice as much in their sweetheart as I can. (Josh Billings, in Myers 1968: 17)
Love may be blind, but it certainly finds its way around in the dark. (Esar 1968: 203)
Love may be blind but it seems to find its way around. (McKenzie 1980: 314)
Never kiss at the garden gate. Love is blind but the neighbours ain't. (Kilroy 1985: 357)
The reason we can't see ourselves as others see us is that love is blind. (Esar 1968: 713)

Love laughs at locksmiths.
(DAP 389; ODEP 491; CODP 158; MPPS 386)
{Nothing can prevent lovers from getting together.}
Love laughs at locksmiths, but not at locks – at least, not at wedlock. (Esar 1968: 492)
Love laughs more often at logic than at locksmiths. (Esar 1968: 485)
What's so funny about locksmiths? (Berman 1997: 248)

Love makes the world go round.
(DAP 389; ODEP 492; CODP 158-159; MPPS 386-387; NTC 142)
{Love keeps things going.}
John - "Yes, I had a little balance in the bank, but I got engaged two months ago, and now--"
Joan - "Ah, love makes the world go round."
John - "Yes, but I didn't think it would go round so fast as to make lose my balance." (Copeland 1965: 208)
Love doesn't make the world go 'round. Love is what makes the ride worthwhile. (Franklin P. Jones, in Prochnow 1988: 176)
Love doesn't really make the world go round. It just makes people so dizzy it looks like it. (McKenzie 1980: 314)
Love makes the bed springs sound. (Liu and Vasselli 1996)
Love makes the world go around
It's just an optical illusion caused by a male and a female going around in circles. (Safian 1967: 21)
Love makes the world go down. (Rees 1981: 79; Kilroy 1985: 386)
Love makes the world go round, and divorce makes it wobble. (Esar 1968: 886)
Love makes the world go round, and so does a good stiff drink. (Esar 1968: 244)
Love makes the world go round, but it's the lack of money that keeps it flat. (Safian 1967: 56)
Love makes the world...spooky! (*Boston Globe*, August 31, 1997: without pages)

Love me, love my dog.
(DAP 391; ODEP 492; CODP 159; NTC 143)
{If you love me, you should accept everyone and everything I love, as well as all my weaknesses and foibles.}
Love me, love my dog.
But me first. (Gerilyse greeting card [Chicago] purchased in February 1996 in Burlington, Vermont)
"Love me, love my doggerel," said the poet to his lady. (Mieder and Kingsbury 1994: 81)

Love your [thy] neighbor as yourself.
(DAP 427)
{Try to get along with people.}
Fear thy neighbor as thyself. (Eugene O'Neill, in Berman 1997: 249)
I'm very religious - which means, of course, that I love my neighbour. Mind you, I really hate her husband. (Metcalf 1993: 180)
It isn't easy to love your neighbor as your pelf. (Herbert V. Prochnow, in Prochnow 1988: 267)
It would be much easier to love our neighbors as ourselves if they would only do things the way we do. (Esar 1968: 546)
It wouldn't be so hard to love our neighbors as ourselves if we didn't dislike them so much. (Esar 1968: 546)
"Love thy neighbor," as the parson said to the man who lived next door to the pigsty. (Mieder and Kingsbury 1994: 80)
Love thy neighbor, but do not make love to her. (Esar 1968: 546)
Love thy neighbor, but don't remove the fence. (Safian 1967: 14)
"Love thy neighbor," but first be sure she isn't married! (McKenzie 1980: 358)
Love thy neighbor, but make sure her husband is away. (Kandel 1976)
Love your neighbor as yourself - but no more. (Mieder 1993: 186)

Love your neighbor, but do not pull down the fence. (DAP 427)
Love your neighbor, but leave his wife alone. (DAP 427)
Love your neighbor, yet pull not down your hedge. (DAP 427)
Love thy neighbour - but don't get caught. (Reisner 1971: 174;
Kilroy 1985: 44)
Love thy neighbour - but make sure his wife doesn't find out.
(Kilroy 1985: 263)
Love thy neighbour - regularly. (Rees 1981: 94)

Make haste slowly.
(DAP 284; ODEP 501; CODP 124; MPPS 289; NTC 145)
{Quick actions may cause failure, so proceed deliberately.}
Make haste slowly...except when killing mosquitoes. (Berman
1997: 182)
Make love slowly! (Kilroy 1985: 237)

Make hay while the sun shines.
(DAP 286; ODEP 501; CODP 161; MPPS 293; NTC 145)
{Take immediate advantage of favorable circumstances.}
Make hay while the sun shines...and make rye while the moon
shines. (Berman 1997: 183)
Make hay while the sun shines
And you'll get a sunstroke. (Safian 1967: 22)
Many a man who makes hay while the sun shines would prefer
to make love while the moon shines. (Esar 1968: 690)

Man does not [cannot] live by bread alone.
(DAP 400; CODP 162; MPPS 396; NTC 146)
{People have not only physical but also spiritual needs.}
After all, one does not live by ties alone. (Countess Mara ties
advertisement). (*New Yorker*, November 22, 1982: 70)
Ford automobiles do not run on gasoline alone. (Ford advertise-
ment). (*Wall Street Journal*, August 10, 1982: 12-13)
Journalists do not live by words alone, although sometimes they
have to eat them. (Adlai Stevenson, in Esar 1968: 447)
Man cannot live by blue jeans alone. (Wrangler advertisement).

WOMAN
CANNOT LIVE
BY DIAMONDS
ALONE.

BILL BLASS
PERFUME FOR WOMEN
at the Ultima II counter

(*Punch*, May 1, 1974: 724-725)

Man cannot live by bread alone, but he manages on just the crust. (Safian 1967: 11)

Man cannot live by clothes alone. (Pierre Cardin man's cologne advertisement). (*New York*, December 11, 1973: 23)

Man cannot live by sex alone. (*Punch*, November 17, 1971: 684; Mieder 1993: 68)

Man cannot live by vitamins alone. He needs minerals, too. (Unicap advertisement). (*Woman's Day*, February 1979: 76)

Man cannot live on bread alone - He needs a bit of crumpet. (Kilroy 1985: 363)

Man can't live on bread alone - he has to have credit cards. (Esar 1968: 191)

Man does not live by BLUE alone. (Levi's jeans advertisement.) (*Brattleboro Reformer*, October 17, 1980: 3)

Man does not live by bread alone...a little butter, an egg, or a chop is also welcome. (Chefs of the West advertisement). (*Sunset*, April 1977: 212)

Man does not live by bread alone, even pre-sliced bread. (Denis W. Brogan, in Esar 1968: 94)

Man does not live by...getting married. (Monteiro 1968: 128)

Man does not live by toast alone. (General Electrics advertisement). (*Better Homes & Gardens*, December 1983: inside back cover; *Woman's Day*, December 13, 1983: 51)

Man lives not by water alone. (Waterford crystal advertisement). (*New Yorker*, February 7, 1977: inside front cover)

Man lives not by Waterford alone. (Waterford crystal advertisement). (*New York Times Magazine*, February 26, 1978: 2; *New Yorker*, March 26, 1979: inside back cover [Aynsler China advertisement]))

Man may not live by bread alone, but many people live chiefly on crust. (Esar 1968: 417)

Man should not live on hamburger alone. (Hillshire Farm sausages advertisement). (*Better Homes & Gardens*, August 1985: 89)

The man who lives by bread alone, lives alone. (Berman 1997:

260)
Traveling man does not live by bed alone. (Stouffer Hotels advertisement). (*Flightime* [*sic*], June 1978: 51; Mieder 1993: 68)
Woman cannot live by diamonds alone. (Bill Blass perfume advertisement). (*New Yorker*, May 25, 1987: inside front cover)

Man proposes, God disposes.
(DAP 401; ODEP 506; CODP 162-163; MPPS 398-399; NTC 146)
{People can make plans but they can't control their outcome.}
Man proposes, and a mother-in-law opposes. (Esar 1952: 220)
Man proposes, and his mother-in-law opposes. (Safian 1967: 29)
Man proposes and marriage exposes. (Esar 1968: 287)
Man proposes, and the computer disposes. (Safian 1967: 29)
Man proposes and the girl weighs his pocketbook and decides. (Loomis 1949: 355)
Man proposes - but not always marriage. (Esar 1968: 641)
Man proposes, then woman imposes. (Wurdz 1904)

Many a true word is spoken in jest.
(DAP 673; ODEP 841; CODP 230; MPPS 699; NTC 146)
{Teasing and joking often have a serious part to them.}
Many a true word is spoken through false teeth. (Esar 1968: 799; Kilroy 1985: 343)
Many a wise word is spoken in ignorance. (Esar 1968: 874)
There's many a knock gits across in a jest. (Kin Hubbard, in Berman 1997: 206)
Too many a word spoken in jest spoils the joke. (Esar 1968: 446)

Many are called but few are chosen.
(DAP 80; CODP 165; NTC 146)
{Though people may want something, only a select few get it.}
Many are called but few are called back. (Berman 1997: 264)
Many are called but few deliver the goods. (Berman 1997: 264)

"Many are called," said Fred,
"But few are chosen."
"And many are cold," said Ned,
"But few are frozen." (Rees 1965: 42)
Speaking of houseguests, Oliver Herford said: "Many are called,
but few get up." (Woods 1967: 325)

Many hands make light work.
(DAP 276; ODEP 509; CODP 165; MPPS 283; NTC 147)
{Large tasks are carried out easier and more quickly when
divided among many people.}
Light work makes many hands worry about layoffs. (Liu and
Vasselli 1996)
Many hands make light work...and a heavy payroll. (Berman
1997: 456)

Marriage is a lottery.
(DAP 406; ODEP 513; CODP 166; MPPS 405)
{You can never say what kind of a spouse your partner is going
to turn out to be.}
If marriage is a lottery, alimony must be a sort of gambling
debt. (Esar 1968: 26)
Marriage is a lottery! Yes, but you can't tear up your ticket if
you lose! (Kilroy 1985: 421)

Marriages are made in heaven.
(DAP 407; ODEP 514; CODP 166; MPPS 405; NTC 147)
{Providence provides the partner.}
Garages are made in heaven. (Farman 1989)
Marriages are made in heaven, but the maintenance work has to
be done on earth. (Safian 1967: 15)
Marriages are made in heaven...but they're broken down here on
earth. (Berman 1997: 264)
Marriages are made in heaven...So is thunder and lightning.
(Berman 1997: 264)

Marry in haste and repent at leisure.
(DAP 407; ODEP 515; CODP 167; MPPS 289; NTC 147-148)
{If you rush into marriage without thinking, you will probably regret the choice for a long time.}
A manuscript is something that is submitted in haste and returned at leisure. (Oliver Herford, in Berman 1997: 265)
Marry in haste, and pay alimony at leisure. (Esar 1968: 26)
Marry in haste, and repeat at pleasure. (Safian 1967: 44)
Marry in haste and repent at our mother-in-law's. (Esar 1968: 534)
Marry in haste and repent in the Divorce Court. (Anonymous 1908: 10)
Marry in haste and repent insolvent. (Safian 1967: 37)
Marry in haste, and you'll never have any leisure to repent in. (Esar 1968: 469)
Marry in Hollywood and repeat indefinitely. (Esar 1968: 388)
Modern version: Marry in haste, repeat at pleasure. (Copeland 1965: 782)
Reform in haste, and repent at leisure. (Esar 1968: 667)
Those who marry in haste often see better bargains at leisure. (Esar 1968: 64)
Used car buyers
Buy in haste and repair at leisure. (Safian 1967: 51)

Men seldom make passes at girls who wear glasses.
(DAP 402)
{Often men appear to be looking only for outside beauty.}
In Hawaii, men make passes at girls who wear grasses. (Henny Youngman, in Berman 1997: 273)
Men always make passes at girls who drain glasses. (Esar 1968: 244)
Men make passes at gals who drain glasses. (Safian 1967: 40)
Men often make passes at girls who hold glasses. (L.L. Levinson, in Berman 1997: 273)
Men seldom make passes at a girl who surpasses. (Franklin P. Jones, in Berman 1997: 273)

When a man makes passes at girls who wear glasses, it's probably due to their frames. (Esar 1968: 345)

Mind your own business.
(DAP 76; ODEP 533; NTC 149)
{Worry about your own affairs and not those of others.}
The man who works for another should not spend too much time minding his own business. (Esar 1968: 104)
The reason some folks can't mind their own business is because they have very little mind and no business. (McKenzie 1980: 57)
There are two reasons why people don't mind their own business: either they haven't any mind, or they haven't any business. (Berman 1997: 42)

Misery loves company.
(DAP 413; CODP 170-171; MPPS 414; NTC 149)
{Unhappy people will get some consolation if they know that others are also unhappy.}
Misery loves company, but can't bear competition. (Josh Billings, in Esar 1968: 522)
Misery loves company
But company doesn't reciprocate. (Safian 1967: 25; Esar 1968: 522)
Misery loves company, but happiness throws more parties. (Esar 1968: 579)
Misery loves company...but it's better to have rheumatism in one leg than both. (Berman 1997: 276)
Misery loves company, but not the company the bill collector works for. (Esar 1968: 78)
Misery loves those "900" psychic and sex phone lines. (Liu and Vasselli 1996)
Misery's love of company oft goeth unrequited. (James Thurber, *The Hen Party*, in Thurber 1956: 73)

Moderation in all things.
(DAP 414; ODEP 520; CODP 152; MPPS 415; NTC 149)

{Try not to overdo things.}
"Be moderate in all things," as the boy said to his schoolmaster when the latter was whipping him. (Mieder and Kingsbury 1994: 85)
Moderation in all things...including moderation? (Berman 1997: 278)
Moderation in all things...said the boy to his father who was about to give his son a spanking. (Berman 1997: 278)

Money can't [doesn't] buy [bring] happiness.
(DAP 416-417; MPPS 416)
{Financial security does not necessarily mean happiness.}
Anyone who says money doesn't buy happiness doesn't know where to shop. (Berman 1997: 282)
Even if money could buy happiness, think what a luxury tax there would be on it. (Adams 1959: 154)
Happiness can't buy money. (Kandel 1976; Kilroy 1985: 202)
Money alone will not bring happiness, but it will attract interesting companions. (McKenzie 1980: 229)
Money cannot buy happiness, but then happiness cannot buy groceries. (Esar 1968: 106)
Money can't buy happiness, but it helps you to be unhappy in comfort. (McKenzie 1980: 229)
Money can't buy happiness, but it helps you to look for it in many more places. (Esar 1968: 369)
Money can't buy happiness. That's why we have credit cards! (Metcalf 1993: 46)
Money can't buy you friends, but it brings you a better class of enemies. (McLellan 1996: 158)
Money doesn't bring happiness - but it does help you look for it in interesting places. (Safian 1967: 53)
Money doesn't bring happiness - but it's marvelous for quieting the nerves. (Safian 1967: 53)
Money doesn't bring happiness - but it's nice to find it out for yourself. (Safian 1967: 53)
Money doesn't bring happiness - but it keeps your creditors in

a better frame of mind. (Safian 1967: 53)
Money may not buy happiness, but most of us are willing to make the experiment. (Esar 1968: 286)
Money won't buy happiness, but it will go a long way in helping you. (DAP 416)
Money won't buy happiness, but it will keep you from being more than moderately sullen and depressed. (McKenzie 1980: 229)
Money won't buy happiness, but it's nice to choose your way to be unhappy. (Mieder 1993: 185)

Money doesn't grow on trees.
(DAP 416; NTC 150)
{It is difficult to get money.}
If money doesn't grow on trees, how come the banks have so many branches? (Metcalf 1993: 19)
Money doesn't grow on trees, but it grows on many family trees. (Esar 1968: 296)
Money doesn't grow on trees, but you can get it out of some sap. (Barbour 1964: 296)
Money doesn't grow on trees...unless you happen to be a successful orchardist. (Berman 1997: 283)

Money [The love of money] is the root of all evil.
(DAP 416-417; ODEP 150; CODP 173; MPPS 387; NTC 150-151)
{All wrongdoing can be traced to the pursuit of riches.}
If money is at the root of all evil, it is also at the root of all morality. (Fuller 1943: 214)
In the underworld, money isn't the root of all evil, but evil is the root of all money. (Esar 1968: 193)
Love of money is the root of half the evil in the world, and lack of money is the root of the other half. (Esar 1968: 277)
Matri-money is the root of all evil. (Anonymous 1908: 26)
Matrimony is the root of all evil. (Edmund and Williams 1921: 275)

Sometimes adversity is the mother of invention.

The invention is the Automatic Shift Lock.

From the beginning, we were confident it could help prevent unintended acceleration in our cars.

Now the National Highway Traffic Safety Administration (NHTSA) has asked us to install it on 250,000 1978-86 Audi 5000s.

Audi owners have also been urged by the NHTSA to have the Shift Lock installed as the best safeguard against unintended acceleration.

Not only have we complied with the government's request, but we will also seek to set a new industry standard for owner participation in a recall.

To that end, we are initiating a program which makes available at participating dealers up to 1,000 Audis to be used by as many of our customers as possible while their Automatic Shift Locks are being installed.

Our responsibility has always been to our customers. Our compliance with this recall, and our effort to develop and install the industry's only real safeguard against unintended acceleration, should satisfy any doubts about Audi.

As the automotive press and thousands of loyal owners attest, the Audi 5000 has been and continues to be one of the finest cars in the world.

BEETLE BAILEY

144

Money is the root of all evil and a man needs roots. (Kandel 1976)
Money is the root of all evil - but has anyone ever discovered a better route? (Safian 1967: 54)
Money is the root of all evil - but it does seem to grow some mighty fine plants. (Safian 1967: 54)
Money is the root of all evil - but it doesn't make it any easier to dig it up. (Safian 1967: 54)
Money is the root of all wealth. (Haan and Hammerstrom 1980)
Money is the root of happiness. (*The Burlington Free Press*, January 5, 1992: without pages)
Money is the root of...the bank of America. (Stark 1982)
Money may be the root of all evil, but if we didn't make it somebody else would. (*New Yorker*, January 30, 1960: 21)
Money roots out all evil. (Rosten 1972: 30)
Monkey is the route to all people. (Rees 1980: 91)
Philanthropy proves that though money is the root of all evil, it is also the route of much good. (Esar 1968: 595)
Remember - Money is the root of all evil. If money is the root of all evil, why does everyone root for it? (*Brattleboro Reformer*, February 28, 1981: 14; Mieder 1989: 274)
Runny is the snoot of all weevils. (Farman 1989)
Television violence is the root of all evil. (Liu and Vasselli 1996)
The lack of money is the root of all evil. (Mark Twain, in Flavell 1993: 170; DAP 416)
The love of evil is the root of all money. (Esar 1952: 85)
The love of money is the root of all evil, except now it isn't around long enough for even a fleeting romance. (McKenzie 1980: 346)
The love of money is the root of all virtue. (Esar 1968: 255)
The love of someone else's money is the root of all evil. (Esar 1968: 528)
With corrupt officials, money is the loot of all evil. (Esar 1968: 96)

Money isn't everything.
(DAP 417; CODP 172; MPPS 417)
{Wealth alone does not bring contentment.}
Always remember that money isn't everything - but also remember to make a lot of it before talking such nonsense! (McKenzie 1980: 343)
Anybody who thinks money is everything has never been sick. (McKenzie 1980: 232)
Money doesn't mean everything in this world, but somehow everything in this world seems to mean money. (Muller 1932: 68)
Money isn't everything - a certified check will do just as well. (Safian 1967: 55)
Money isn't everything - but it comes in pretty handy if you've mislaid your credit card. (Safian 1967: 55)
Money isn't everything, but it does quiet the nerves a little. (McKenzie 1980: 344)
Money isn't everything, but it sure keeps you in touch with the children. (McLellan 1996: 160)
Money isn't everything, but it's a long way ahead of whatever comes next. (Metcalf 1993: 148)
Money isn't everything - but it's a nice consolation until you have everything. (Safian 1967: 55)
Money isn't everything, but it's certainly handy if you don't have a credit card. (Metcalf 1993: 148-149)
Money isn't everything, but it's the best substitute for credit. (Esar 1968: 775)
Money isn't everything, but it's way ahead of any of its competitors. (Esar 1968: 529)
Money isn't everything - but it's way ahead of whatever is in second place. (Safian 1967: 55)
Money isn't everything, but subtract it from some people and there's nothing left. (Esar 1968: 528)
Money isn't everything. I've had money and I've had everything - and believe me, they're not the same. (Metcalf 1993: 148)
Money isn't everything; in fact, after the tax collector gets

through, money isn't anything. (Esar 1968: 528)
Money isn't everything - in fact, with taxes and the high cost of living, it's nothing. (Safian 1967: 55)
Money isn't everything. It isn't even enough. (Kilroy 1985: 306)
Money isn't everything - only half. (Feibleman 1978: 16)
Money isn't everything - sometimes it isn't even enough. (Safian 1967: 55)
Money isn't everything - there are other things besides money, like stocks, bonds, travelers' checks, and credit cards. (Safian 1967: 55)
Money isn't everything. There's also credit cards and traveler's cheques. (Metcalf 1993: 148)
Money isn't everything – there's always diamonds. (Esar 1968: 218)
Money isn't everything.
Who told you that?
My boss. (Metcalf 1993: 149)
Money may not be everything, but it's a pretty good cure for poverty. (Mieder 1993: 36)
Our parents used to tell us that money isn't everything. Now we tell our kids that money isn't *anything*. (Metcalf 1993: 118)
The man to whom money isn't everything, should marry the woman to whom everything isn't money. (Esar 1968: 162)

Money makes the mare go.
(DAP 417; ODEP 539; CODP 173-174; MPPS 418)
{If you have money, you can obtain everything.}
Money makes the mare go...and woman makes the money go. (Berman 1997: 287)
Money makes the mare go, but horses make the money go. (Anonymous 1908: 25)
Money makes the mare go...but it's credit that runs the automobile. (Berman 1997: 287)
Money makes the mare go, but not if it's bet on her. (Esar 1968: 396)
Money makes the mare go - but not the nightmare. (Mieder

1993: 185)
Money makes the mayor go. (Wurdz 1904)
Money makes the nightmare go. (*New Yorker*, June 28, 1956)

Money talks.
(DAP 417; CODP 174; MPPS 418)
{Money is the most influental and important thing in the world.}
If campaign money talks, it is careful not to tell where it came from. (McKenzie 1980: 347)
If money really talked it might make interesting remarks about the people who have it. (Esar 1968: 436)
It's true that money talks, but nowadays you can't hold on to it long enough to start a conversation. (McKenzie 1980: 345)
Money doesn't really talk; it just makes a sonic boom as it goes by. (McKenzie 1980: 344)
Money doesn't talk - it just goes without saying. (Esar 1968: 758)
Money may talk, but have you ever noticed how hard of hearing it is when you call it? (Fuller 1943: 214)
Money may talk but it seems to be very hard of hearing when you call it. (Adams 1959: 154)
Money no longer talks - it just gasps. Many people can hear its death rattle! (McKenzie 1980: 346)
Money still talks, of course, but it has to stop and catch its breath more often. (McKenzie 1980: 343)
Money talks...and a lack of it talks even louder. (Berman 1997: 290)
Money talks - and mostly it says "good-bye." (Safian 1967: 55)
Money talks, but big money doesn't - it hires a staff of lawyers. (Esar 1968: 465)
Money talks, but campaign money is careful not to tell where it came from. (Esar 1968: 262)
Money talks - but it also stops talk. (Safian 1967: 55; Esar 1968, 81)
Money talks, but it doesn't always talk sense. (Esar 1968: 529)
Money talks, but it doesn't always tell the truth. (Esar 1968:

148

474)
Money talks, but it doesn't say when it's coming back. (McLellan 1996: 159)
Money talks, but it rarely gives itself away. (Esar 1968: 595)
Money talks but nobody notices what kind of grammar it uses. (Anonymous 1908: 10)
Money talks, but not when it's a small amount. (Esar 1968: 528)
Money talks - but the folks who know how to accumulate it, don't. (Safian 1967: 55)
Money talks, but the people who want their money talk the loudest. (Esar 1968: 192)
Money talks - but who can hold on to it long enough to start a conversation? (Safian 1967: 55)
Money talks - but with the dollar so depreciated, it no longer talks common cents. (Safian 1967: 55)
Money talks these days, but its list of speaking acquaintances is growing narrower and more exclusive. (McKenzie 1980: 345)
The important thing is not that money talks, but that it has the largest listening audience. (Esar 1968: 50)
They say money talks. But smart money listens. (Dresdner Bank advertisement). (*Business Week*, October 19, 1981: 152; Mieder 1989: 274)
United States money not only talks - it has learned - to speak every foreign language. (Adams 1959: 154)
When money talks it often merely remarks 'Good-by.' (*Saturday Evening Post*, Sept. 5, 1903)
"Yes, money talks - which means it can lie." (*New Yorker*, August 18, 1997: 55)

Nature abhors a vacuum.
(DAP 424; ODEP 55; CODP 178; MPPS 440; NTC 153)
{There is always something to fill a void.}
Nature abhors a vacuum, and human nature abhors a whore. (Esar 1968: 642)
Nature abhors a vacuum and she sometimes fills an empty head with conceit. (Herbert V. Prochnow, Sr., in Prochnow 1988:

269)
Nature abhors a vacuum: when a head lacks brains, she fills it with conceit. (Esar 1968: 840)

Necessity is the mother of invention.
(DAP 425; ODEP 558; CODP 179; MPPS 441; NTC 153)
{A need encourages creative ways to be figured out.}
A condom is the mother of all prevention. (Liu and Vasselli 1996)
At Smith Corona simplicity is the mother of invention. (Smith Corona advertisement). (*New Yorker*, August 22, 1988: 3)
"Boredom, like necessity, is very often the mother of invention." (Mingo and Javna 1989: 68)
If necessity is the mother of invention, she must be worried about having so many children that won't work. (Esar 1968: 441)
Ignorance is the mother of admiration. (George Chapman, in Berman 1997: 297)
Invention is the mother of necessity. (Samuel Butler, in Adams 1969: 250)
Necessity is a mother. (Kandel 1976)
Necessity is often the mother of invention, but more often she is childless. (Esar 1968: 545)
Necessity is the martyr of invention. (Safian 1967: 46)
Necessity is the mother of contention. (Anonymous 1908: 26)
Necessity is the mother of convention. (Kilroy 1985: 175)
Necessity is the mother of intervention. (Esar 1968: 40)
Necessity is the mother of invention, but to many a necessity is the mother of tension. (Esar 1968: 545)
Necessity is the mother of invention, especially the invention of lies. (Esar 1968: 544)
Necessity is the mother of "taking chances." (Mark Twain, in Prochnow 1988: 347)
Necessity is the mother of tension. (Safian 1967: 44)
Necessity may have been the mother of invention, but today invention is the mother of necessities. (Esar 1968: 440)

Obesity is the mother of invention. (Metcalf 1993: 57)
Said Father, as he tried to think up a new excuse for being out late, "Mother is the necessity for invention." (*Life*, ca. 1925, in Berman 1997: 298)
Sometimes adversity is the mother of invention. (Audi advertisement). (*Time*, February 2, 1987: 23; Mieder 1989: 315)
When children ask embarrassing questions, invention is the necessity of mother. (Esar 1968: 263)

Necessity knows no law.
(DAP 425; ODEP 557-558; CODP 179; MPPS 441; NTC 153-154)
{In need someone might be forced to do unusual or even illegal things.}
As a student in law school, they called him "Necessity" because he knew no law. (Braude 1955: 220)
Necessity knows no law, and neither does the average lawyer. (McKenzie 1980: 294)
Necessity knows no law, and the man who practices law seldom knows necessity. (Esar 1968: 463)
Necessity knows no law, but it is intimately acquainted with many lawyers. (DAP 363, 425)
The trial had been proceeding for some time and every one was amused by one lawyer's consistently referring to the opposing lawyer as "Mr. Necessity." After awhile, the judge inquired, "May I ask, Mr. Jackson, why you always refer to learned councel as 'Mr. Necessity'?" "Simply, Your Honor," was the reply, "because he knows no law." (Esar 1945: 303)

Neither a borrower nor a lender be.
(DAP 63; NTC 154)
{Don't borrow money or lend it.}
A borrower is the thing to be, since one can file for bankruptcy. (Liu and Vasselli 1996)
Neither a borrower nor a lender be...but if you must do one, lend. (Josh Billings, in Berman 1997: 35)

Neither a borrower nor a lender be...unless the interest rates are in your favor. (Berman 1997: 35)

Never [Don't] look a gift horse in the mouth.
(DAP 311; ODEP 301; CODP 105; MPPS 324-325; NTC 71)
{Don't be too critical of a gift you get.}
Never let a gift horse in the house. (Rosten 1972: 30)
Never look a gift cigar in the label. (Loomis 1949: 356)
Never look a gift horse in the mouth, especially if it be the Colt revolver. (Loomis 1949: 356)

Never [Don't] put off till [until] tomorrow what you can do today.
(DAP 603; ODEP 656; CODP 210; MPPS 636; NTC 71-72)
{If something needs to be done, do it straight away without procrastination.}
A bill collector doesn't believe in putting off until tomorrow what can be dunned today. (Esar 1968: 78)
A neurotic never puts off till tomorrow the worrying she can do today. (Esar 1968: 547)
A procrastinator is one who puts off until tomorrow the things he has already put off until today. (McKenzie 1980: 424)
A woman never puts off till tomorrow what she can say today. (Esar 1968: 791)
Always put off till tomorrow what you might rue today. (Esar 1968: 668)
Always put off till tomorrow what you shouldn't be doing today. (Safian 1967: 34)
Always put off till tomorrow what you shouldn't do at all. (Esar 1968: 620)
Chorus girls
Never leave off till tomorrow what you can take off today. (Safian 1967: 47)
Don't do today what you can put off until tomorrow. (DAP 601)
Don't put off till tomorrow what you can put off till next week. (Barbour 1964: 297)

Don't put off today what you can't put off tomorrow. (DAP 601)
Don't put off until tomorrow what...you put on to go to bed.
(Stark 1982)
Many a woman never puts off till tomorrow the gossip she can
spread today. (Esar 1968: 353)
Never do today what can be done tomorrow. (DAP 601)
Never do today what you can get somebody else to do tomor-
row. (DAP 601)
Never pull off tomorrow what you can pull off today. (Reisner
1971: 150)
Never put off till tomorrow the favor someone is willing to do
for you today. (Esar 1968: 303)
Never put off 'till tomorrow what you can avoid altogether.
(Kandel 1976)
Never put off till tomorrow what you can do today, unless
someone else did it yesterday. (Esar 1968: 620)
Never put off till tomorrow what you can get someone else to do
for you today. (Esar 1968: 815)
Never put off till tomorrow what you can put over today. (Safian
1967: 34)
Never put off till tomorrow what you shouldn't be doing at all.
(Safian 1967: 34)
Never put off until tomorrow what you can do the day after
tomorrow. (Mark Twain, in Metcalf 1993: 173)
Never put off until tomorrow what you can put off for good.
(Metcalf 1993: 173)
Never put off until tomorrow what your secretary can do today.
(Berman 1997: 348)
Put not off till tomorrow what can be enjoyed today. (Josh
Billings, in Berman 1997: 348)

Never underestimate the power of a woman [women].
(DAP 478)
{Women have more strength and influence than some people
want to admit.}
Never underestimate the power of a woman – nor overestimate

Never underestimate the power of an Opel.

Introducing the special edition fuel-injected Opel. Face it. We're a nation that's grown up on big cars and big engines. The idea of a small, economical car with real underhood wizardry is still something of an enigma to us.

So, when you decide to purchase the new fuel-injected Opel, be prepared to handle a barrage of inquiries from "Where's the carburetor?" to "What'll she do?" to "Howzit work?".

But it isn't actually how fuel injection works that's important. It's what it does. And what it does is take a car with supple suspension, with front and rear stabilizer bars,

with reclining bucket seats, with meticulous engineering—and transform it into something with real response when you prod the throttle.

The new fuel-injected Opel. It's a beautiful little piece of machinery. But when you go tooling around in one, be prepared. The local

assortment of car buffs may want to ask you a few questions.

Dedicated to the Free Spirit in just about everyone.

154

her age and weight. (Esar 1968: 274)
Never underestimate the power of an antenna. (Hirschmann antenna advertisement). (*Ms.*, December 1977: 79)
Never underestimate the power of an Opel. (Opel advertisement). (*Time*, June 30, 1975: 42)
Never underestimate the power of...termites. (Stark 1982)
Never underestimate the powers of the obstinate sex. (Safian 1967: 45)

No man can [A man cannot] serve two masters.
(DAP 402; ODEP 569; CODP 183; MPPS 399; NTC 157)
{You cannot work for two different employers or purposes and be faithful to both.}
It is easier to serve two masters than to master two servants. (Esar 1952: 84)
No man can serve two masters...or mistresses. (Berman 1997: 266)
No man can serve two masters, unless he has a wife and grown-up daughter. (Esar 1968: 721)
No man can serve two masters; yes-men can serve hundreds. (Braude 1955: 237)

No man is a hero to his valet.
(DAP 299; ODEP 570; CODP 183; MPPS 399)
{No one is more aware of someone's failings and faults than the subordinate.}
A valet's testimony tells you more about valets than heroes. (Leo Rosten, in Berman 1997: 189)
Every man is a hero except those who have valets. (Esar 1968: 382)
No author is a hero to his proofreader. (Esar 1968: 383)
No man is a hero to a bill collector. (*Louisville Times*, ca. 1925, in Berman 1997: 189)
No man is a hero to his mother-in-law. (Esar 1952: 220; Henny Youngman, in Berman 1997: 189)
No man is a hero to his press agent. (Esar 1968: 629)

"No man is a hero to his valet." Heroes never have valets. (Hubbard 1973: 49)

No man is a hero to his wallet. (Safian 1967: 40; Copeland 1965: 794)

No man is a hero to his wife's lawyer. (Esar 1968: 382)

No man is a hero to his wife's psychiatrist. (Eric Berne, in Berman 1997: 189)

No news is good news.
(DAP 429-430; ODEP 572; CODP 184; MPPS 445; NTC 157)
{Without information about something or somebody, we can safely assume that all is well.}

No gnus is good gnus. (*The Burlington Free Press*, December 14, 1974: 19)

No news is good news; no journalists is even better. (Nicolas Bentley, in Prochnow 1988: 25)

No news is...impossible. (Stark 1982)

"No noose is good news," as the man said when reprieved. (Mieder and Kingsbury 1994: 89)

No nudes is good news. (*Chicago Tribune Magazine*, December 30, 1973: 15)

No nukes is good nukes. (Nierenberg 1994: 551)

Nobody is perfect.
(DAP 431; MPPS 449)
{No human being is without faults.}

No body is perfect. (The Lean [exercising] Machine advertisement). (*Time*, April 9, 1984: 9; Mieder 1989: 275)

No one is perfect, except the man who makes a perfect fool of himself. (Esar 1968: 319)

Wife (heatedly) - "You're lazy, you're worthless, you're bad-tempered, you're shiftless, you're a thorough liar."
Husband (reasonably) - "Well, my dear, no man is perfect." (Copeland 1965: 227)

Nobody's prefect. And to err is human. (New England Telephone advertisement). (Burlington [Vt.] mailing from June 1984)

None but the brave deserve the fair.
(DAP 67; CODP 29; NTC 158)
{Only courageous people deserve to get the best.}
None but the brave can live with the fair. (Safian 1967: 29)
None but the brave desert the fair. (Esar 1968: 1)
None but the brave deserve affairs. (Safian 1967: 29, 46; Berman 1997: 37)
None but the brave deserve the fair, but only the rich can support them. (Esar 1968: 784)
Only the brave dare ask the fare. (J. Hobday, in Berman 1997: 37)

Nothing is certain but death and taxes.
(DAP 89, 139; ODEP 580; CODP 185-186; MPPS 158; NTC 160)
{We can't be sure in anything.}
"Ah, me!" moaned Brown after he had had another disappointment. "Nothing is certain in this world but death and taxes." "That's true enough," agreed Black, "but at least death doesn't get worse every time Congress meets." (Esar 1945: 442)
Another difference between death and taxes is that death is frequently painless. (McKenzie 1980: 124)
Death and taxes are inevitable, but death is not a repeater. (McKenzie 1980: 497)
Death and taxes may be the only certainties in life, but nowhere is it written that we have to tax ourselves to death. (*Nation's Business*, in Prochnow 1988: 412)
Nothing is certain but death and higher taxes. (Esar 1968: 120)
Nothing is certain but debt and taxes. (Esar 1968: 120)
Nothing is certain in this world except death, taxes, and teen-agers. (McKenzie 1980: 124)
The way they are driven, nothing is more certain than death in taxis. (Esar 1968: 796)

Nothing succeeds like success.
(DAP 571; ODEP 581; CODP 187; MPPS 453-454; NTC 161)

{Success breeds more success.}
Moderation is a fatal thing: nothing succeeds like excess. (Oscar Wilde, in Esar 1968: 526)
Nothing fails like success. (G. K. Chesterton, in Berman 1997: 393)
Nothing recedes like success. (Safian 1967: 41; Walter Winchel, in Metcalf 1993: 206)
Nothing succeeds like excess. (Safian 1967: 39; Shaw 1980)
Nothing succeeds like success, and nothing fails like reading a book on how to attain it. (Esar 1968: 779)
Nothing succeeds like success - but an inheritance from a rich relative doesn't hurt either. (Safian 1967: 14)

Nothing ventured [venture], nothing gained [had; won; have].
(DAP 630; ODEP 581; CODP 187; MPPS 454; NTC 161)
{If you don't take risks, you will never get anything.}
Nothing risqué, nothing gained. (Safian 1967: 41)
Nothin' tried, nothin' got away with. (*The Burlington Free Press*, April 11: 1975: 30)
Nothing ventured, nothing sprained. (Safian 1967: 48)
Nothing vouchered, nothing gained. (Berman 1997: 307)

Of two evils choose the less(er) [least].
(DAP 186; ODEP 233; CODP 83; MPPS 206; NTC 203)
{When faced with two unpleasant options, choose the less damaging one.}
A pessimist is a man who doesn't choose the lesser of two evils, but both. (Esar 1968: 591)
A press agent never choses the lesser of two evils, but the one most likely to be talked about. (Esar 1968: 629)
Between two evils, choose neither; between two goods, choose both. (McKenzie 1980: 159)
Instead of choosing the lesser of two evils, choose the one you haven't tried before. (Esar 1968: 276)
Of two evils, choose neither. (Charles H. Spurgeon, in Ridout and Witting 1969: 132)

Of two evils, choose the more enjoyable. (Berman 1997: 122)
Of two evils choose the one least likely to be talked about.
(Anonymous 1908: 24)
Of two evils, choose the one with the better-looking legs. (Esar
1968: 469)
Of two evils, choose the prettier. (Esar 1968: 276)
Of two evils choose to be the least. (Bierce 1958: 120)
Of two evils, it isn't always possible to choose the lesser -
sometimes they are twins. (Esar 1968: 830)
Pessimist: one who, when he has the choice of two evils,
chooses both. (Prochnow 1988: 426)
When choosing between two evil alternatives, I usually take the
one I've never tried before. (Yu and Jang 1975: 106)

Old soldiers never die (, they simply fade away).
(DAP 551; MPPS 581)
{As people get older they tend to lose in importance.}
Contestant: "You know, bankers never die, they just lose
interest."
Groucho Marx: "Not the bankers I know. They'd rather die than
lose any interest." (Mingo and Javna 1989: 18)
Old accountants never die; they just lose their balance. (Anony-
mous 1965: 290)
Old female lawyers never die; they just lose their appeals.
(Berman 1997: 379)
Old fishermen never die - they just smell that way. (Rees 1980:
58)
Old gardeners never die. They just spade away and then throw
in the trowel. (Herbert V. Prochnow, Sr., in Prochnow 1988:
265)
Old golfers never die. They just tee off and putt away. (McKen-
zie 1980: 212)
Old jokes never die, they just end up in every comic's brain file.
(Adams 1959: 95)
Old physicians never die; they just lose their patients. (Berman
1997: 379)

Old politicians never die - they just run once too often. (McKenzie 1980: 401)

Old postmen never die. They just lose their zip. (McKenzie 1980: 410)

Old principals never die; they just lose their faculties. Old teachers never die; they just lose their principals. (Anonymous 1965: 290)

Old quarterbacks never die; they just fade back and pass away. (McKenzie 1980: 476)

Old rugby players never die. They simply have their balls taken away. (Kilroy 1985: 361)

Old salesmen never die - they just get out of commission. (McKenzie 1980: 458)

Old soldiers never die - just young ones. (Metcalf 1993: 223)

Old soldiers never die. Nor do they go away. (*The Burlington Free Press*, February 22, 1991: 8A)

Old soldiers never die; they just run for political office, command huge lecture fees, or sign lucrative book deals. (Liu and Vasselli 1996)

Old soldiers never die; they just smell that way. (Anonymous 1965: 290; DAP 551)

Television is a form of entertainment where old movies never die, no matter how long ago they were shot. (Esar 1968: 802)

One good turn deserves another.
(DAP 619; ODEP 325; CODP 114; MPPS 651; NTC 163)
{A kindness is repaid in return.}

Among women drivers, one bad turn deserves another. (Esar 1952: 215)

One delicious secret deserves another. (Hidden Valley salad dressing advertisement). (*Bon Appétit*, May 1981: 105; Mieder 1989: 274)

One good beer...deserves another. (Heineken advertisement). (*New Yorker*, September 17, 1979: 94-95; *Newsweek*, November 5, 1979: 102-103)

One good Butterball deserves another. (Butterball Turkeys

advertisement). (*The Burlington Free Press*, November 14, 1978: 6D)

One good lie requires another. (Esar 1968: 474)

One good Scotch deserves another! (Black & White advertisement). (*New Yorker*, August 7, 1965: 11)

One good taste deserves another. (Natural Light Beer advertisement). (*Sports Illustrated*, October 19, 1981: 60; Mieder 1989: 274)

"One good turn deserves another," as the alderman said when he discharged the thief who voted for him. (Mieder and Kingsbury 1994: 143)

"One good turn deserves another," as the dog said, chasing his tail. (Mieder and Kingsbury 1994: 143)

"One good turn deserves another," said the customer, as he padded the chorus girl's tights. (Mieder and Kingsbury 1994: 143)

One good turn gets the whole blanket. (Safian 1967: 35)

One good turn-on deserves another. (Reisner 1971: 126)

One great vegetable deserves another. (*Better Homes & Gardens*, September 1988: 188)

One romantic setting deserves another. (Royal Doulton advertisement). (*Bon Appétit*, May 1985: 15; Mieder 1989: 275)

One man's loss is another man's gain.
(DAP 386; ODEP 486; CODP 139; MPPS 400; NTC 164)
{Sometimes we benefit from another person's misfortune.}

One man's junk is another man's antique. (Safian 1967: 30)

One man's loss is another man's umbrella. (Safian 1967: 30)

One man's stumbling block is another man's stepping-stone. (Berman 1997: 241)

"One man's theft is another man's justice." (Mingo and Javna 1989: 224)

One man's trash is another man's treasure. (Berman 1997: 241)

One man's wage rise is another man's price increase. (Harold Wilson, in Berman 1997: 241)

162

One man's meat is another man's poison.
(DAP 408; ODEP 522; CODP 168; MPPS 400; NTC 165)
{What might be good for one person might well be bad for
another.}
News item: Pope rules that whale meat is fish, for fast-day
purposes. One man's meat is another man's *poisson*. (Berman
1997: 267)
One man's corn is another man's bourbon. (Esar 1968: 181)
One man's drive is another man's funeral. (Safian 1967: 30)
One man's fish is another man's *poisson*. (Carolyn Wells, in
Esar 1952: 96)
One man's mate is another man's passion. (Loomis 1949: 355)
One man's mate is another man's poison. (Safian 1967: 31)
One man's mate may sometimes be another man's prison. (James
Thurber, *The Bachelor Penguin and the Virtuous Mate*, in Thur-
ber 1956: 83)
One man's meat is another man's cholesterol. (Safian 1967: 30)
One man's meat is another man's perversion. (Reisner 1971:
144)
One man's meat is another man's poisson. (Farman 1989)
One man's meat may become another man's poison if it's not
cooked well enough. (Liu and Vasselli 1996)
One man's nerve is another man's nervousness. (Safian 1967:
30)
One man's success is another man's failure. (*St. Louis Post-Dis-
patch*, December 29, 1974: no pages)
One man's sushi is another man's steak. (Japan Air Lines adver-
tisement). (*Gourmet*, September 1974: 69)
One woman's poise is another woman's poison. (Safian 1967:
30; McKenzie 1980: 398)

One [A] picture is worth a [ten] thousand words.
(DAP 463; CODP 201; NTC 11)
{A visual image conveys information more effectively than
words.}
A Cross says more than a thousand kisses. (Cross pens advertise-

"And I say one bomb is worth a thousand words."

One man's <u>sushi</u>
is another man's steak.

There's just no second guessing about taste. So, to keep everyone happy, we have a simple solution.
Two cuisines.
One is Japanese.
The other is Continental.
No matter which one you choose—the familiar or the adventurous—one thing remains the same: the elegant, understated service that is ours alone.
It's reflected in the smile of your JAL hostess as she offers you a steaming oshibori towel to refresh yourself. Her

delicate grace as she pours your sake. The very special way she makes you feel like an honored guest at a family banquet.
Unique service like this doesn't just happen at mealtime. From our first hello to our last sayonara, we do our best to prove there's as much difference between airlines as between airline menus.
We're the one where East meets West.

JAPAN AIR LINES

ment). (*Punch*, December 10, 1986: 40)

A flower is worth a thousand words. (American Florist advertisement). (*Family Circle*, January 24, 1984: 36; Mieder 1989: 275)

A hug is worth a thousand words. (1980 poster by Argus Communications [Niles, Illinois]; Mieder 1993: 144)

A picture is worth a thousand words, especially if the picture is by Picasso. (Esar 1968: 598)

A picture is worth a thousand words. I guess Shakespeare should have learned to draw. (Mieder 1993: 142)

A picture used to be worth a thousand words - then came television. (Esar 1968: 599)

A pitcher [of beer] is worth a thousand words. (*Bloomington Herald Telephone*, October 27, 1982: 34; Mieder 1989: 274)

A word that's worth a thousand pictures. Vermont. (Howard Bank advertisement). (*The Burlington Free Press*, March 2, 1978: 12A)

"And I say one bomb is worth a thousand words." (*New Yorker*, April 14, 1980: 52)

Brazil: One visit is worth a thousand words. (Brazilian Tourism Authority advertisement). (*Saturday Review*, March 20, 1976: 37)

In an argument with a man, one sniffle is worth a thousand words. (Esar 1968: 797)

Ireland: A place that's worth a thousand pictures. (Ireland advertisement). (*Newsweek*, March 31, 1980: 53)

One dollar is worth a thousand words. (*New Yorker*, December 7, 1987: 52)

One drive is worth a million words. (Jaguar advertisement). (*Punch*, May 10, 1972: 639)

One drive is worth a thousand words. (Thunderbird advertisement). (*New Yorker*, August 20, 1984: 94a; *Time*, September 3, 1984: 43; Mieder 1989: 275)

One flower can speak a thousand words. (Recycled Paper Products [Chicago] greeting card purchased in February 1989 in Burlington, Vermont)

These words are worth a thousand pictures.

Rather than a lot of interesting photos, we offer you one very interesting fact: Merit delivers the taste of cigarettes that have up to 38% more tar. The secret is Enriched Flavor.™ It gives Merit real, satisfying cigarette taste, but with even less tar than other leading lights. But don't take our word for it. Try one yourself. You'll get the picture.

Enriched Flavor,™ low tar. A solution with Merit.

MERIT
Filter

One good developer is worth a million words. (Westwood Building advertisement). (*Punch*, October 31, 1973: iii)

One look is worth a thousand words. (Street Railways Company advertising). (*Printers' Ink*, December 8, 1921: 96-97)

One picture is worth a thousand faxes. (*The Burlington Free Press*, June 3, 1995: 1C)

One picture is worth a thousand hamburgers. (Business Committee for the Arts advertisement). (*Time*, July 15, 1985: 6; Mieder 1989: 275)

One picture may be worth ten thousand words, but some advertisers believe in using both in the same ad. (McKenzie 1980: 10)

One sound is often worth 2,000 pictures. Hearing is believing. (NBC Radio Network advertisement). (*Fortune*, November 6, 1978: 129)

One taste is worth a thousand pictures. (Danish Blue Cheese advertisement). (*New Yorker*, February 9, 1957: 115; *Bon Appétit*, September 1983: 76 [Great Cheeses of Europe advertisement]; Mieder 1989: 275)

One touch is worth a thousand words. (Angostar warmbody underwear advertisement). (*Skiing Trade News*, Spring 1980: 34-35)

Sometimes a word is worth a thousand pictures. (Fortune magazine advertisement). (*Fortune*, February 11, 1980: 18)

The picture says a thousand words but the sound will leave you speechless. (Panasonic advertisement). (*New Yorker*, September 2, 1985: 90)

These words are worth a thousand pictures. (Merit cigarettes advertisement). (*Time*, October 24, 1988: back cover)

One swallow does not make a summer.
(DAP 575-576; ODEP 791; CODP 247; MPPS 607; NTC 165-166)
{A single piece of evidence doesn't prove anything.}
One swallow doesn't make a summer - but a pair of baby-blue eyes can make a fall. (Safian 1967: 16)

One swallow doesn't make a summer, but it breaks a New Year's resolution. (Edmund and Williams 1921: 147)
One swallow doesn't make a summer - but too many swallows make a fall. (Safian 1967: 16; George D. Prentice, in Adams 1969: 99)
"One swallow does not make a summer."
"Very true, but several swallows of liquor frequently make a fall." (Copeland 1965: 126)

Opportunity knocks but once.
[Opportunity [fortune] never knocks twice at any man's door; Opportunity seldom knocks twice].
(DAP 440; ODEP 282; CODP 194; MPPS 464; NTC 166-167)
{You should take full advantage of an opportunity, for you may never get another chance.}
Because opportunity rarely rings twice. (Bell Telephone advertisement). (*New Yorker*, May 24, 1982: 119; Mieder 1989: 274)
Even when opportunity knocks, a man still has to get off his seat and open the door. (McKenzie 1980: 7)
For the modern girl, opportunity doesn't knock. It parks in front of her home and honks the horn. (McKenzie 1980: 204)
Fortune knocks but once at any man's door, but misfortune has much more patience. (Esar 1968: 523)
If opportunity came in the form of a temptation, knocking once would be sufficient. (McKenzie 1980: 373)
Knock!
Who's there?
Opportunity! (Dundes 1966: 510)
Opportunity always knocks at the least opportune moment. (Berman 1997: 313)
Opportunity does not batter the door off its hinges when it knocks. (McKenzie 1980: 373)
Opportunity doesn't knock for people who don't give a rap. (Esar 1968: 564)
Opportunity doesn't knock. *You* knock, opportunity answers. (Berman 1997: 313)

168

Opportunity has to knock, but it is enough for temptation to stand outside and whistle. (McKenzie 1980: 374)

Opportunity knocks but once, but for a pretty girl it whistles all the time. (Esar 1968: 865)

Opportunity knocks but once, but temptation hammers incessantly. (DAP 440)

Opportunity knocks but once; trouble is more persistent. (Esar 1968: 590)

Opportunity knocks but once...while trouble calls on the telephone. (Berman 1997: 313)

Opportunity knocks for a man, but woman gets a ring. (Barbour 1963: 100)

Opportunity knocks once, and the neighbors the rest of the time. (Copeland 1965: 782; Safian 1967: 12)

Opposites attract.
(DAP 441; MPPS 464)
{Sometimes unlike people or things go together.}

Opposites attract...but similarities endure. (Leo Rosten, in Berman 1997: 314)

Opposites attract: many a man has a brunette wife and a blonde sweetheart. (Esar 1968: 83)

Opposites attract – that's why so many men are attracted to girls with money. (Esar 1968: 565)

Out of sight, out of mind.
(DAP 540; ODEP 602; CODP 195; MPPS 566; NTC 167)
{Absent people or things are soon forgotten.}

Out of sight, only in mind. (Wurdz 1904)

"Out of sight, out of mind," said the warden as the escaped lunatic dissappeared over the hill. (Mieder and Kingsbury 1994: 120)

Out of the mouths of babes (comes truth).
(DAP 33; CODP 176; NTC 168)
{Children often tell the truth when adults would never tell it.}

Out of the mouths of babes come remarks their parents should
never have uttered in the first place. (Safian 1967: 37)
Out of the mouths of babes come words we adults should never
have said. (Esar 1968: 674)
You know what they say: out of the mouths of babes
comes...cereal. (Metcalf 1993: 17)

Patience is a virtue.
(DAP 453; ODEP 613; CODP 197-198; MPPS 476; NTC 169)
{It is good to be able to wait for positive events or things.}
Patience is a virtue...but sometimes a sign that you just don't
know what to do. (Berman 1997: 317)
Patience is a virtue...but you've got to have a lot of patience to
acquire it. (Berman 1997: 317)
Patience is a virtue which few possess - some have a little,
others have less. (DAP 453)

Penny-wise, pound-foolish.
(DAP 458; ODEP 620; CODP 200; MPPS 482; NTC 170)
{Don't be thrifty with small amounts of money and foolish with
large sums.}
Come be pennywise, while our pound is being foolish. (British
Airways advertisement). (*New Yorker*, August 16, 1976: 5)
Don't be penny-wise and sound foolish. (Bose stereo advertise-
ment). (*National Lampoon*, April 1974: 38; *New York Times
Magazine*, April 24, 1977 [TDK Electronics advertisement]: 62;
Mieder 1989: 303)
Many a man manages to be pound-foolish without being penny-
wise. (Esar 1968: 757)
Penny wise and gowned foolish. (Safian 1967: 44)
There's a pen for the wise, but alas! no pound for the foolish!
(Anonymous 1908: 19)

People who live in glass houses shouldn't throw stones.
(DAP 252-3; ODEP 360; CODP 106; MPPS 484; NTC 170)
{Do not criticize or slander another person for having the same

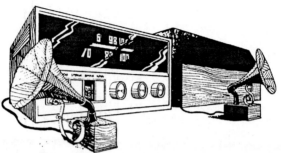

"Don't be penny-wise and sound foolish"

If you've priced hi-fi components lately, you probably think you have to spend a small fortune to obtain a quality home music system, right? Well, depending on how much you're willing to invest, it's possible to keep some of the cost down without any real sacrifice in audible quality.

A rule of thumb to consider is that you should plan on investing at least 50% of your hi-fi equipment

"budget" on your speaker system. Because if your speakers are not able to deliver clean, lifelike music reproduction, well, you just won't hear the true beauty of the music you enjoy, regardless of how much you spend on a receiver or turntable.

You can hear what this means by trying a brief experiment at any of your nearby authorized BOSE dealers. Just ask to hear our moderately priced BOSE 501 SERIES II Direct/Reflecting® speakers compared to the sound reproduction you hear with any other speakers up to the cost of the 901 SERIES II. Chances are the sound of the 501 with inexpensive accessory components will save you money you thought you'd have to spend on a more expensive receiver and turntable!

So, whatever your budget, don't be penny-wise and sound foolish. Try our little experiment and you're sure to put your money where your speakers are. Of course, the BOSE 901® system may be just the best choice for you, if you're willing to spend more.

For more information on the BOSE 901 and 501 SERIES II speakers, write Dept. LN, BOSE Corporation, The Mountain, Framingham, MA., 01701.

BOSE 501 SERIES II

faults that you yourself have.}

"People in stucco houses should not throw quiche." (Mingo and Javna 1989: 207)

People that live in glass houses should not take a bath. (Barbour 1963: 100; Barbour 1964: 296)

People that live in glass houses should pull down the shades when they get dressed. (Barbour 1963: 100; Barbour 1964: 296)

People who live in gall bladders shouldn't throw stones. (Safian 1967: 32)

People who live in glass houses had better draw the drapes. (Safian 1967: 32)

People who live in glass houses make the most interesting neighbors. (Esar 1968: 546)

People who live in glass houses might as well answer the doorbell. (Safian 1967: 32; Metcalf 1993: 111)

People who live in glass houses should dress in the dark. (Wurdz 1904)

People who live in glass houses should have Levelor Blinds. (Levelor Blinds advertisement). (*Better Homes & Gardens*, December 1982: 82)

People who live in glass houses should raise flowers. (Esar 1968: 316)

People who live in glass houses should screw in the basement. (Kilroy 1985: 281)

People who live in glass houses should take out insurance. (Esar 1968: 433; Metcalf 1993: 122)

People who live in glass houses shouldn't. (Safian 1967: 32)

People who live in glass houses shouldn't expect to do much living. (Safian 1967: 32)

People who live in glass houses shouldn't get stoned. (Rosten 1972: 32; Shaw 1980)

People who live in stone houses shouldn't throw glasses. (Kandel 1976)

People who love in glass houses should pull down the blinds. (Anonymous 1908: 27)

People who manage glass buildings shouldn't throw energy out the window. (Independence Heating advertisement). (*Time*, April 6, 1981: 44)

Pitchers who live in glass houses shouldn't throw fastballs. (*The Burlington Free Press*, February 5, 1993: 10A)

Remember, those who live in grass houses shouldn't throw spears. (*Brattleboro Reformer*, March 30, 1990: 19)

T-shirt: People who live in glass blouses shouldn't show bones. (Kilroy 1985: 85)

Physician, heal thyself.
(DAP 462; ODEP 622; CODP 201; MPPS 486; NTC 170)
{Before blaming or correcting someone, first make sure you don't have the same faults or problems yourself.}

Physician, heal thyself because your colleages can't afford malpractice insurance. (*The Burlington Free Press*, June 3, 1995: 1C)

Physician, heal thyself...Your doctor doesn't make house calls either. (Berman 1997: 327)

Physician, inform thyself. (*Time*, June 26, 1989: 71)

Physician, jog thyself. (*Punch*, January 14, 1987: 29)

Politics makes strange bedfellows.
(DAP 472; ODEP 535; CODP 204; MPPS 504; NTC 170-171)
{Political interests can bring together people who otherwise dislike and avoid each other.}

Divorce makes estranged bedfellows. (Berman 1997: 335)

Marriage makes strange bedfellows. (Berman 1997: 335)

Politicians

Politics makes estranged bedfellows. (Safian 1967: 49)

Politics doesn't make strange bedfellows - marriage does. (Groucho Marx, in Esar 1968: 70)

Politics makes strange bad fellows. (Esar 1968: 616)

Politics makes strange bedfellows, and so does prostitution. (Esar 1968: 642)

Politics makes strange bedfellows, but they are always willing to lie on their own side. (Esar 1968: 616)

THE FAR SIDE by Gary Larson

"OK, Zukutu — that does it! Remember, those who live in grass houses shouldn't throw spears."

"Physician, jog thyself!"

The bedfellows politics makes are never strange. It only seems that way to those who have not watched the courtship. (McKenzie 1980: 405)

Possession is nine [eleven] points of the law.
(DAP 475; ODEP 640; CODP 204-205; MPPS 505; NTC 171)
{If a full legal right to something has not been established, the person who is in possession of it has a greater right to it than somebody else who claims it.}
In a dictatorship, suppression is nine points of the law. (Esar 1968: 219)
In court, wrangling between lawyers is nine points of the law. (Esar 1968: 186)

Practice makes perfect.
(DAP 479; ODEP 856; CODP 206; MPPS 509; NTC 171)
{The only way to master any skill is to do it over and over again.}
Cab drivers are living proof that practice does not make perfect. (Howard Ogden, in Berman 1997: 340)
If you think practice makes perfect, you don't have a child taking piano lessons. (Berman 1997: 340)
Practice does not make a lawyer perfect, but enough of it will make him rich. (McKenzie 1980: 295)
Practice makes perfect, but with lawyers it is more likely to make them rich. (Esar 1968: 465)
Practice makes perfect...when you practice perfection. (Berman 1997: 340)
Practiss makes perfict. (Kandel 1976)
Practice makes pervert. (Reisner 1971: 144)
Praktiss makes purfikt. (Kilroy 1985: 241)
Praxis makes perfect. (Olivetti typewriter advertisement). (*New Yorker*, March 8, 1982: 99)

Practice what you preach.
(DAP 479; ODEP 643; CODP 206; MPPS 510; NTC 171-172)

{Do yourself what you advise other people to do.}
A clergyman is a man whose mother practices what he preaches.
(Esar 1968: 143)
If some persons preached what they practiced, they would have
to be censored. (Esar 1968: 416)
Practice what you preach...said the wife of the minister, re-
minding him to rehearse his sermon. (Berman 1997: 340)

Pride goes [goeth; comes] before a fall.
[Pride will have a fall].
(DAP 483; ODEP 647; CODP 207; MPPS 511; NTC 172)
{Arrogant or overconfident people are likely to make mistakes
leading to their fall.}
Pride goeth before a fall, but it goeth a lot quicker after one.
(Esar 1968: 630)
Pride goeth before destruction, except in the dictionary. (Esar
1968: 630)
"Pride must have a fall," exclaimed a mechanic, as he knocked
down a dandy who had abused him. (Mieder and Kingsbury
1994: 100)

Procrastination is the thief of time.
(DAP 485; ODEP 648; CODP 208; MPPS 512; NTC 172-173)
{Procrastination usually ends up in nothing being done properly
or accomplished at all.}
Procrastination is the thief of time, and the loot can never be
recovered. (Esar 1968: 621)
Procrastination is the thief of time. So are a lot of other big
words. (McKenzie 1980: 424)
Procreation is the thief of time. (Rees 1980: 103)

Revenge is sweet.
(DAP 507; ODEP 673; CODP 214; MPPS 530; NTC 177)
{It is very pleasurable to get even.}
A Chicago man calls his sweetheart Revenge because she is so
sweet. (Esar 1952: 156)

If revenge is sweet, why does it leave such a bitter taste? (McKenzie 1980: 451)

"Revenge is sweet," as the boy said who had been whipped by a grocer while he was stealing his sugar. (Mieder and Kingsbury 1994: 132)

Revenge is sweet...but not when you're on the receiving end. (Berman 1997: 357)

Revenge is sweet, but not when you're the victim. (Esar 1968: 844)

Rome wasn't built in a day.
(DAP 515; ODEP 683; CODP 217-218; MPPS 535; NTC 178)
{It takes a lot of time and hard work to obtain important results.}
One afternoon in ancient Rome another housewife complained to her husband that there was no water in the house. He angrily turned on her and shouted, "Remember, woman, *Rome wasn't built on a bay*." (Howard 1989: 257)

Rome was not built in a daze. (Loomis 1949: 356)

Rome wasn't built in a day, probably because it was a government job. (Esar 1968: 691)

Rome wasn't built in a day - they had their labor troubles too. (Esar 1968: 691)

Rome wasn't burned in a day. (Rosten 1972: 33)

Save for a rainy day.
(DAP 136; ODEP 663; MPPS 154-155; NTC 179)
{Save your money to meet possible emergencies in the future.}
A miser begins by saving up for a rainy day, and ends by saving up for the rainy days of his heirs. (Esar 1968: 522)

Attention girls: Always save a boyfriend for a rainy day - and another one in case it doesn't rain. (McKenzie 1980: 204)

Folks who saved for a rainy day are deluged by annoying drips who didn't. (McKenzie 1980: 515)

Have you put anything away for a rainy day?
Yes, my wellingtons [boots]. (Metcalf 1993: 187)

In England, saving for a rainy day and saving for a holiday are

usually the same thing. (Metcalf 1993: 72)
Many a man who saves up for a rainy day is frustrated to find
he has to put a new roof on his house. (Esar 1968: 673)
One thing most children save for a rainy day is lots of energy.
(McKenzie 1980: 70)
Rainy days come to those who save up for them. (Esar 1968:
660)
Some people are so stingy you'd think they were saving their
money for a rainy century. (Esar 1968: 767)
What a mother should save for a rainy day is patience. (McKen-
zie 1980: 348)
What a small boy saves for a rainy day is apt to be mischief.
(McKenzie 1980: 52)

See no evil, hear no evil, speak no evil.
(DAP 187; CODP 24; MPPS 421; NTC 179)
{Ignore any evil you may come in contact with. The proverb is
often represented by three monkeys, one of which is covering his
eyes, one his ears, and one his mouth.}
Ask no gays. See no gays. Hear no gays. (*Los Angeles Times*,
July 20, 1993: 7B)
"Behind the Iron Curtain"
Speak no facts, see no facts, hear no facts. (*Saturday Review*,
February 25, 1950: 10)
Disunited Nations Week
I saw no good, I heard no good, I said no good, I want no good,
I am up to no good. (*Time*, October 25, 1943: 29)
Hear no compromise, see no compromise, speak no compromise.
(*Punch*, June 8, 1966: 827)
Hear no diesel. See no diesel. Smell no diesel. (*Observer*, De-
cember 30, 1990: 14)
Hear no evil, see no evil, and speak no evil, and you'll never be
a success at a cocktail party, or as a best-selling author. (Safian
1967: 11)
Hear no gold. See no gold. Speak no gold. (*New York Times*,
May 12 12, 1997: without pages)

Of course,
that leaves
"DO NO EVIL"
wide open!

HAVE FUN!

ON YOUR BIRTHDAY,

Hear no evil, speak no evil, see no evil...

Hear no military, see no military, speak no military. (*Atlanta Journal & Constitution*, December 15, 1985: 3C)

I hear no evil, and see no evil - two out of three ain't bad. (Berman 1997: 122)

If you think no evil, see no evil, and hear no evil, the chances are that you'll never write a best-selling novel. (Prochnow 1988: 441)

On Your Birthday.
Hear no evil, speak no evil, see no evil.
Of course, that leaves "Do no evil" wide open!
Have fun! (Hallmark greeting card, purchased in February 1981 in Burlington, Vermont)

See no evil, hear no evil, speak no evil, have no fun. (Mieder 1987: 175)

See no evil - Taste no evil - Smell no evil. (*Fortune*, October 1941: 6)

See no fascist evil, speak no fascist evil, hear no fascist evil. (*Los Angeles Times*, May 29, 1981: part II, 7)

See no full price. Hear no full price. Speak no full price. (Barneys clothes advertisement). (*New York Times*, November 30, 1997; 3)

See no homework! Hear no homework! Speak no homework! (Hallmark greeting card, purchased in June 1986 in Burlington, Vermont)

See no problem (except for Japan [says General Motors]). Speak no problem (except for Japan [says Ford]). Hear no problem (except for Japan [says Chrysler]). (*Los Angeles Times*, January 12, 1992: M5)

Speak no evil, see no evil, hear no evil - and you'll never be the life of the party. (Esar 1968: 276)

Speak no evil, see no evil, hear no evil - and you'll never write a bestseller. (Esar 1968: 74)

Speak no tax hike, hear no tax hike, see no tax hike - until after the election, of course. (*Los Angeles Times*, July 27, 1984: part II, 5)

The fourth monkey: eat no evil. (*New Yorker*, July 20, 1992: 63)

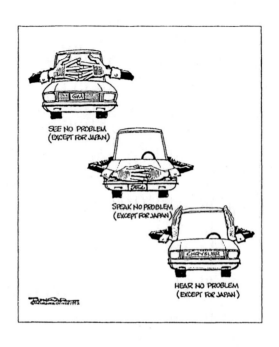

Seeing is believing.
(DAP 530; ODEP 710; CODP 225; MPPS 551-552; NTC 179-180)
{You can believe something is true just after you have seen its evidence with your own eyes.}
Feeling is believing. (Southwick Clothes advertisement). (*New Yorker*, December 14, 1963: 71)
Hearing is believing! (Western Electric vacuum tubes advertisement). (*Time*, December 1940: 75; *Fortune*, November 6, 1978: 129 [NBC Radio Network advertisement])
If some skeptics thought seeing is believing, they wouldn't look. (Esar 1968: 739)
Seeing is believing and buying! (Tri-State Plastic Molding advertising). (*Fortune*, April 1955: 192)
Seeing is believing, but don't bet on another man's game. (Berman 1997: 368)
Seeing is believing, but not when you're looking at a television commercial. (Esar 1968: 156)
Tasting is believing. (Diet Rite Cola advertisement). (*Brattleboro Reformer*, December 8, 1980: 12; *New Yorker*, September 9, 1985: 81 [Perugina chocolate advertisement])

Seek and you [ye] shall find.
[Seek and you shall find; knock, and it shall be opened unto you].
(DAP 530-531; ODEP 711; CODP 225; MPPS 552; NTC 180)
{In order to get something, one has to put some efforts into looking for it.}
Seek, and ye shall find; knock, and nothing shall be opened unto you. (Hubbard 1973: 90)
Seek and ye shall find that a lot of other people are looking for the same thing. (Berman 1997: 368)
Sneak and ye shall find. (Berman 1997: 368)

Silence gives consent.
(DAP 540; ODEP 733; CODP 229-230; MPPS 567; NTC 183)

Tasting is believing.

Here's a coupon to help you do it. Until you do, you won't believe any diet cola can taste this good. Less than a calorie a serving. More great cola taste. Diet Rite Cola, ya got what it takes!

Ya got great taste goin' for you!

{If you do not say anything, you can be assumed to have no objection.}
"Silence gives consent," as the man said when he kissed the dumb woman. (Mieder and Kingsbury 1994: 120)
Silence gives contempt. (Berman 1997: 372)
When you are climbing a mountain, don't talk; silence gives ascent. (Robert J. Burdett, in Berman 1997: 372)

Silence is golden.
(DAP 540; CODP 229; MPPS 586; NTC 184)
{It is good at times not to say anything.}
If silence is golden, not many people can be arrested for hoarding. (McKenzie 1980: 467)
Silence is golden, especially for the blackmailer. (Esar 1968: 81)
Silence is golden...Maybe that's why it's so rare. (Berman 1997: 372)
The only golden thing that some women dislike is silence. (Esar 1968: 348)

Slow but [and] sure [steady] (wins the race).
[Slowly but surely.]
(DAP 547; ODEP 743, 744; CODP 232; MPPS 575; NTC 184-185)
{Consistent effort, patience and perseverance lead to success.}
Many men are slow but sure. Others are just slow. (McKenzie 1980: 332)
Slow and steady may win the race, but history records that the tortoise won only one race with the hare. (Esar 1968: 743)

Spare the rod and spoil the child.
(DAP 514; ODEP 759; CODP 236; MPPS 534; NTC 187)
{When misbehaving, children need physical punishment, otherwise they will grow up spoiled and will expect everyone to indulge them.}
An Irishman in maternity ward is worried that the thin and sickly baby he sees is his own. "No," says the nurse, pointing to a fine,

chubby, baby boy, "this is yours; the other child was born by artificial insemination." "Just what I've always heard said: 'Spare the rod and spoil the child'." (Legman 1968: 589)

Don't spare the rod, or you may some day find junior carrying one. (Esar 1968: 650)

Spare the brush and save the hair. (*Boston Sunday Globe (My Parade)*, December 16, 1973: 5)

Spare the rod and save the child. (Hubbard 1973: 150)

Spare the rod – and you'll get struck by lightning. (Esar 1968: 479)

Spare the rod and you'll have no fish for dinner. (Loomis 1949: 357)

Spare the rod, lose the child. (*Maine Sunday Telegram*, August 11, 1996; 3C)

Spare the rules, spoil the child. (*Punch*, December 23, 1981: 1141)

Spoil the rod and spare the child. (William Dean Howells, in Esar 1968: 422)

Speak well of the dead.
[Never speak ill of the dead].
(DAP 137; ODEP 761; CODP 237; MPPS 156-157; NTC 156)
{There is no use in speaking ill of people who cannot defend themselves.}

If we were to speak only well of the dead, history would be even falser than it is now. (Esar 1968: 386)

Some people never say anything bad about the dead, or anything good about the living. (McKenzie 1980: 41)

They say you shouldn't say anything about the dead unless it's good.

He's dead? Good! (Metcalf 1993: 53)

Sticks and stones may break my bones, but words will never hurt me.
(DAP 563; ODEP 773; CODP 240; MPPS 594-595; NTC 240)

Spare the rules, spoil the child.

A child is sometimes the most susceptible and vulnerable consumer of all. Which is why any advertising aimed at children needs tight control. Hence the rules on the right.

These are just some of the rules affecting children's advertising and they appear in a book called the British Code of Advertising Practice. In it are many rules, not just affecting children's advertising. They govern all advertisements which appear in the press, or in direct mail, in print, on posters and cinema commercials.

The Code is used by the Advertising Standards Authority whose job it is to protect the public from unacceptable advertising. (To help us interpret and develop the Code, we have recently carried out research into children's reactions to advertisements.)

Amongst other things, the ASA responds to consumers' complaints, and this briefly is the way the system works. Members of the public can write to us to complain about any advertisement they find unacceptable. If, after investigation, we find the advertisement contravenes the Code, we instruct the advertiser to amend or withdraw the advertisement.

Appendix B Children

General 1.1 Direct appeals or exhortations to buy should not be made to children unless the product advertised is one likely to be of interest to them which they could reasonably be expected to afford for themselves.

1.2 Advertisements should not encourage children to make themselves a nuisance to their parents, or anyone else, with the aim of persuading them to buy an advertised product.

1.3 No advertisement should cause children to believe that they will be inferior to other children, or unpopular with them, if they do not buy a particular product, or have it bought for them.

1.4 No advertisement for a commercial product should suggest to children that, if they do not buy it or encourage others to do so, they will be failing in their duty or lacking in loyalty.

1.5 Advertisements addressed to children should make it easy for a child to judge the true size of a product (preferably by showing it in relation to some common object) and should take care to avoid any confusion between the characteristics of real-life articles and toy copies of them.

1.6 Where the results obtainable by the use of a product are shown, these should not exaggerate what is attainable by an ordinary child.

1.7 Advertisements addressed to children should wherever possible give the price of the advertised product.

Safety 2.1 No advertisement, particularly for a collecting scheme, should encourage children to enter strange places or to converse with strangers in an effort to collect coupons, wrappers, labels or the like.

2.2 Children should not appear to be unattended in street scenes unless they are obviously old enough to be responsible for their own safety; should not be shown playing in the road, unless it is clearly shown to be a play-street or other safe area; should not be shown stepping carelessly off the pavement or crossing the road without due care; in busy street scenes should be seen to use the zebra crossings when crossing the road; and should be otherwise seen in general, as pedestrians or cyclists, to behave in accordance with the Highway Code.

2.3 Children should [...] windows or [...]

2.4 Small children [...] or reaching [...]

2.5 Medicines, [...] should not b[...] parental sup[...] shown using [...]

2.6 Children sh[...] paraffin, pet[...] could lead t[...] injury.

2.7 Children sh[...] machines (e[...] to encourag[...] and Welfare [...]

2.8 An open fi[...] always have [...] the scene.

If you would like to know more about the Code on advertisements addressed to children, or about us, or if you have any cause to complain about an advertisement, we'd like to hear from you.

If an advertiser breaks one of the rules, we won't let him get off lightly.

The Advertising Standards Authority. If an advertisement is wrong, we're here to put it right.

ASA Ltd, Brook House, Torrington Place, London WC1E 7HN.

186

{Don't care about someone's verbal abuse.}
A sadomasochist's secret: Sticks and stones will break my bones,
but whips and chains excite me. (Berman 1997: 388)
Sticks and stones will break your bones, but...not if you hide.
(Stark 1982)

Still waters run deep.
[Still water runs deep].
(DAP 642; ODEP 774; CODP 240-241; MPPS 666; NTC 188)
{A person's calm exterior may conceal profoundness, great depth
of character, emotions or feelings.}
Still water runs deep...and dirty. (Berman 1997: 436)
Still water runs deep...Nonsense; still water doesn't run at all.
(Berman 1997: 436)
Still waters run deep - but how can they run if they are still?
(Esar 1968: 856)
Still waters run deep, but the devil's at the bottom. (Slung 1986:
81)

Strike while the iron is hot.
(DAP 334; ODEP 781; CODP 243-244; MPPS 338-339; NTC
189)
{Take advantage of an opportunity while it lasts.}
Not only strike while the iron is hot, but make it hot by striking.
(DAP 334)
Strike while the boss has a lot of irons in the fire. (Safian 1967:
40)
Strike while the irony is hot. (Safian 1967: 37)
Strike while your employer has a big contract. (Bierce 1958:
120; Barbour 1963: 99)
Striking while the iron is hot may be all right, but don't strike
while the head is hot. (McKenzie 1980: 23)
Women's lib slogan: Don't iron while the strike is hot! (Berman
1997: 390)

Take care of your pennies and the pounds [the dollars] will take care of themselves.
(DAP 458; ODEP 798; CODP 200; MPPS 481)
{If you take care of small amounts of money you will inevitably have a larger sum.}
Count your pennies and the taxes will take care of themselves. (Anonymous 1961: 200)
Save your pennies and the sales tax will take care of them. (McKenzie 1980: 497)
Save your pennies, and your wife's dressmaker will take care of the pounds. (Anonymous 1908: 21)
Take care of the luxuries, and the necessities will take care of themselves. (Esar 1968: 495)
Take care of the pennies and the dollars will take care of your heirs and their lawyers. (Esar 1952: 230; Safian 1967: 56; Prochnow 1988: 432)
Take care of your character and your reputation will take care of itself. (McKenzie 1980: 446)
Take care of your pennies, and the high cost of living will take care of your dollars. (Esar 1968: 699)

Talk is cheap.
(DAP 581; CODP 249-250; MPPS 612; NTC 191)
{Words don't count much without action.}
Anybody who thinks talk is cheap has never argued with a traffic cop. (Berman 1997: 398)
Next time a man tells you talk is cheap, ask him if he knows how much a session of Congress costs. (Esar 1968: 170)
Talk is cheap, but it takes money to buy bread and butter. (Barbour 1964: 297)
Talk is cheap, but it takes money to buy land. (DAP 581)
Talk is cheap, but it takes money to buy liquor. (DAP 581)
Talk is cheap, but it takes money to buy whisky. (Barbour 1964: 297; DAP 581)
Talk is cheap, but not if you say it with flowers. (Esar 1968: 316)

Talk is cheap, but not on the long-distance telephone. (Esar 1968: 800)

Talk is cheap - do something. (McLellan 1996: 4)

Talk is cheap, except when you're talking to a traffic cop. (Esar 1968: 820)

Talk is cheap - until it gets into love letters. (Safian 1967: 15)

Talk is cheap, until you call a lawyer. (Metcalf 1993: 132)

The man who said "talk is cheap" never had a wife with a charge account in a department store. (Braude 1955: 253)

The best things in life are free.
(DAP 49; CODP 17; MPPS 618; NTC 194)
{The most important things do not cost any money and can't be bought for any money.}

If the best things in life are free, why is the family budget so hard to balance? (Esar 1968: 327)

Not all the best things in life are free. (Chival Regal advertisement). (*Gourmet*, April 1974: 7)

The best things in life are duty free. (Rees 1980: 22)

The best things in life are expensive. (Amway advertisement). (*Time*, March 3, 1975: 5)

The best things in life are fleas. (*Brattleboro Reformer*, August 25, 1989: 21)

The best things in life are for fee. (Kandel 1976)

The best things in life are freaky. (Kehl 1977: 289)

The best things in life are free - also the worst advice. (McKenzie 1980: 13)

The best things in life are free, but it costs a lot of time and money before you find this out. (Esar 1968: 183)

The best things in life are free, but the lawmakers are working overtime on the problems. (Safian 1967: 13)

The best things in life are free... but the second best can run into real money. (Berman 1997: 149)

The best things in life are free, but the trouble is that the next best are so expensive. (Esar 1968: 284)

The best things in life are free... for thirty days or your money

DENNIS THE MENACE HANK KETCHAM

"YOU SAY THE BEST THINGS IN LIFE ARE FREE,
BUT GUMBALLS STILL COST A NICKEL."

The proof is in the puffing.

We're not just blowing smoke. Merit delivers remarkably
rich and satisfying tobacco taste. In fact, the majority of smokers
in a nationwide test agreed that Merit tastes as good as or better than
cigarettes that have up to 38% more tar. All this from a cigarette that has even
less tar than other leading lights. The secret is Enriched Flavor.™ Only
Merit has it. But just light one up. It's all the evidence you'll need.

Enriched Flavor,™ low tar. A solution with Merit.

MERIT

190

back. (Liu and Vasselli 1996)
The best things in life are free - including the worst advice.
(McKenzie 1980: 304)
The best things in life are free, of course, but isn't it a pity that
most of the next best things are so expensive? (McKenzie 1980:
112)
The best things in life are frequently expensive. (North Star
Blankets advertisement). (*New Yorker*, October 21, 1961: 184)
The best things in life are three: faith, hope and charity. (Esar
1968: 293)
The lawyer agrees with the doctor that the best things in life are
fees. (McKenzie 1980: 396)
"You say the best things in life are free, but gumballs still cost
a nickel." (*Washington Post*, May 8, 1998: 2E)

The bigger they are, the harder they fall.
(DAP 51; CODP 22; MPPS 45; NTC 194)
{The more prominent people are, the more dramatic is their
failure.}
As she got off at the station,
Polly said to Paul,
"The bigger the summer vacation,
The harder the fall." (Rees 1965: 77)
The bigger they are, the harder they hit. (Weller 1982)
The bigger they are, the harder they maul. (Kandel 1976)
The bigger they come, the more tabloids there are to exploit
their downfall. (Liu and Vasselli 1996)

The child is father of the man.
(DAP 96; ODEP 119; CODP 43; MPPS 111; NTC 196)
{The child's character indicates what sort of person it will be
when it grows up.}
The child is father of the man...unless the offspring happens to
be a girl. (Berman 1997: 54)
The child is father to the man, but there's no second manhood
for second childhood. (Esar 1968: 715)

The child is father to the man, except when the child is a girl. (Esar 1968: 344)

The course of true love never did run smooth.
(DAP 390; ODEP 148; CODP 51-52; MPPS 15; NTC 196)
{People who love each other often have to overcome obstacles in order to be together.}
The course of true love never runs - it stops and parks! (McKenzie 1980: 314)
The course of true love never runs smooth – it usually leads to marriage. (Esar 1968: 491)
The course of two loves never does run smooth. (Copeland 1965: 790; Safian 1967: 42)

The customer is always right.
(DAP 132; CODP 55; MPPS 145; NTC 196-197)
{People who serve customers must always obey their wishes.}
A salesman in a department store was fired because he had been rude to a customer. Some weeks later the store manager noticed him on the street in a police uniform. "Well, Brown, how do you like this job?" he asked him. "Like it?" was the answer. "This job is the answer to a salesman's prayers. It's the only job I know of where the customer is always wrong." (Esar 1945: 114)
Psychiatry is the only business where the customer is always wrong. (McKenzie 1980: 429)
The customer is always right – until his bill is overdue. (Esar 1968: 77)

The devil can quote [cite] scripture for his purpose.
(DAP 146; ODEP 180; CODP 60-61; MPPS 161-162; NTC 197)
{Evil-doing can sometimes be covered up by a high-sounding rationale (quoting persuasive passages of the Bible).}
The devil can cite Scripture for his purpose...He must have gone to Sunday school. (Berman 1997: 89)

The devil can quote Shakespeare for his purpose. (George Bernard Shaw, in Berman 1997: 89)

The early bird catches the worm.
[It is the early bird that catches the worm].
(DAP 52; ODEP 211; CODP 73; MPPS 49-50; NTC 199)
{In order to achieve your goal, get up early in the morning and take full advantage of an opportunity without delay.}
A father exhorting his son to rise early in the morning reminded him of the old adage, "It's the early bird that picks up the worm."
"Ah," replied the son, "But the worm gets up earlier than the bird." (Walsh 1892)
"And remember, my son," said the father of the groom, "the early husband gets his own breakfast." (Copeland 1965: 238)
"Does the early fish get the worm, too, Dad?" (*The Burlington Free Press*, September 16, 1991: 4D)
Early birds get the best buys. (Milot Real Estate advertisement). (*The Burlington Free Press*, December 13, 1981: 11E)
If the early bird gets the worm, then the early cat should get the bird. (*The Burlington Free Press*, December 2, 1986: without pages)
If you don't like worms, what's the sense of being the early bird? (Herbert V. Prochnow, Sr., in Prochnow 1988: 266)
If you must rise early, be sure you are a bird and not a worm. (Esar 1968: 250)
It is not the early bird that catches the worm, but the smart one. (DAP 52)
It is the late husband that catches the lecture. (Loomis 1949: 354)
It's the early girl that catches the coachman. (Loomis 1949: 354)
"Now that I've gotten the worm and since it's still early, I think I'll go back to sleep." (*Ladies' Home Journal*, March 1977: 78)
The early bird catches pneumonia. (Loomis 1949: 354)
The early bird catches the bus. (*The Burlington Free Press*, July 25, 1998: 4C)

The early bird catches the early worm. (Kandel 1976)
The early bird catches the worm - but who wants worms? (DAP 52)
The early bird catches the worm you know....But if I wait another hour I can have shredded wheat. (*Brattleboro Reformer*, September 3, 1983: 19; Mieder 1989: 275)
The early bird gets to Bloomingdale's today to catch the super savings on spring sportswear for misses and juniors. (Bloomingdale advertisement). (*New York Times*, April 15, 1976: 13)
The early bird gets up to serve his wife breakfast in bed. (Safian 1967: 35)
The early bird not only gets the worm but also gets the parking place before you do. (Esar 1968: 577)
The early worm gets eaten by a bird. (Weller 1982)

The end justifies the means.
(DAP 179; ODEP 220; MPPS 200; NTC 199)
{If your purpose is good and noble, in order to reach it you may justify any means, however questionable they might be.}
A home-made dress looks sew-sew.
The ends justify the jeans. (Kilroy 1985: 405)
Shapely slacks wearers
The end justifies the jeans. (Safian 1967: 49)
With some people, the means justify the end; with others, the end justifies the meanness. (Esar 1968: 510)

The family that prays together stays together.
(DAP 198; CODP 90; NTC 200)
{Religious living is good for family life.}
Comes autumn, the family that rakes together aches together. (Berman 1997: 133)
Families that pray together stay together, and families that work together - eat. (McKenzie 1980: 176)
If you go to the beach just remember that the family that bakes together aches together. (McKenzie 1980: 175)
Mafia - the family that preys together. (Berman 1997: 133)

Nowadays the family that buys together cries together. (McKenzie 1980: 111)
The family that lays together stays together!
The family that shoots together loots together!
The family that kicks together sticks together! (Kilroy 1985: 36)
The family that prays together stays together -
thank God my mother-in-law's an atheist. (Rees 1981: 50)
The family that pulls taffy together sticks together. (Berman 1997: 133)
The family that stays together probably has only one car. (Esar 1968: 296; McKenzie 1980: 33)

The good die young.
(DAP 258; CODP 112; MPPS 263; NTC 201)
{Only in youth do people seem to be good and innocent.}
If the good die young, what's the use of making New Year's resolutions? (Esar 1968: 677)
On seeing a grandmotherly face crowned by jet-black hair: Only the young dye good. (Berman 1997: 171)
Only the young die good. (Safian 1967: 37; Oliver Herford, in Woods 1967: 473)
The good die young and, if epitaphs tell the truth, the bad live forever. (Esar 1968: 272)
The good die young - because they see it's no use living if you've got to be good. (Woods 1967: 473)
The good die young, but the bad live on and run for office. (Esar 1968: 109)
The good die young -
Here's hoping you live to a ripe old age. (Prochnow 1988: 423)
The good die, of loneliness. (Safian 1967: 14)
The good die young...particularly if their parents get drunk and neglect them. (Ambrose Bierce, in Berman 1997: 171)
The good die young was never said of a joke. (Fuller 1943: 170)
The good who do not die young get over it. (Esar 1968: 352)
To say the good die young is a standing invitation for the small boy to be bad. (Esar 1952: 86)

The grass is always greener on the other side of the fence.
(DAP 265; CODP 115-116; MPPS 268-269; NTC 202)
{People are permanently dissatisfied, thinking that others have better circumstances or benefit from something more than they do.}
Amca International: Making the grass grow greener on both sides of the fence. (Amca advertisement). (*Wall Street Journal*, November 15, 1977: 7)
Don't envy your neighbor whose grass is greener – his water bill is higher too. (Esar 1968: 357)
Grass is always sweeter when a stranger offers to share some with you. (Liu and Vasselli 1996)
Peas are always greener on the other side of the table. (*The Burlington Free Press*, March 27, 1991: 13A)
The breasts on the other side of the fence look greener. (Feibleman 1978: 73)
The curious thing about grass is that it grows greener on the other side of the fence, but grows faster on your side. (Esar 1968: 357)
The grass always looks greener in the other guy's kitchen. (*The Burlington Free Press*, February 20, 1976: 24)
The grass is always greener on the other fellow's grave. (Rees 1979)
The grass is always greener on the other side of the fence... but their water bill is bigger. (Berman 1997: 173)
The grass is always greener over the septic tank. (Erma Bombeck, *The Grass is Always Greener over the Septic Tank*. New York: McGraw-Hill, 1972)
The grass is greener on the other side of the border. (Nierenberg 1994: 552)
The grass may be greener across the street, but watch out for the barbed wire. (DAP 265)
The grass may seem greener on the other side but it still needs mowing. (James Dobson, in Flavell 1993: 117)
The grass next door may be greener, but it's just as hard to weed. (Esar 1968: 861)

ERMa BoMBecK

THe GRass is ALWaYs GReeNeR OVeR THe SePTic TaNK

The hand that rocks the cradle rules the world.
(DAP 276; ODEP 347; CODP 121; MPPS 282; NTC 202)
{Mothers who look after their children and shape their personalities have the most power and influence.}
Baby-sitter: The hand that rocks the cradle raids the refrigerator. (Berman 1997: 177)
Hubby was very fond of quoting proverbs. So one evening as he sat idly watching his wife trying to put the fretful baby to sleep, he remarked cheerily, "Don't get annoyed, dear. Just remember that, 'The hand that rocks the cradle rules the world'." "That's wonderful," said the wife wearily. "Suppose you step over here and rule the world a while and let me rest." (Esar 1945: 351)
On the matrimonial sea, the hand that rocks the cradle seldom rocks the boat. (McKenzie 1980: 325)
The hand that cooks the meal is the hand that rules the world. (Anonymous 1908: 23)
The hand that rocks the cradle is usually too busy washing dishes to bother about ruling the world. (Esar 1968: 231)
The hand that rocks the cradle rules the world
Lots of babies must be rocking themselves nowadays. (Safian 1967: 23)
The hand that rules the cradle rocks the world. (Peter De Vries, in Esar 1968: 533)
The hand that rules the press rules the country. (Esar 1968: 628)
The hand that signs the cheque book rules the world. (Anonymous 1908: 56)
The hand that used to rock the cradle is now busy writing about planned parenthood. (Esar 1968: 80)

The Lord gives [giveth], and the Lord takes [taketh] away.
(DAP 385; MPPS 259)
{God's will is not be questioned.}
Providence giveth and the income tax taketh away. (Esar 1968: 418)
"The bus bringeth and the bus taketh away. You know, that's a lot like life." (Mingo and Javna 1989: 120)

The Lord giveth, and the IRS [Internal Revenue Service] taketh away. (McKenzie 1980: 269)
The Lord giveth, but since the Lord also taketh away, why is blessed the name of the Lord? (Feibleman 1978: 108)

The meek shall inherit the earth.
(DAP 409)
{The day of improvement will come for the weak and disadvantaged.}
Blessed are the censors for they shall inhibit the earth. (Safian 1967: 41)
Blessed are the meek for they shall inherit the earth - after all the other people in the world are dead. (Esar 1968: 813)
Blessed are the meek for they shall inherit the earth - less 40 percent inheritance tax. (McKenzie 1980: 329)
Blessed are the pure for they shall inhibit the earth. (Esar 1968: 651)
Blessed are the teenagers, for they shall inherit the national debt. (McKenzie 1980: 126)
Blessed are the young, for they shall inherit the national debt. (Herbert C. Hoover, in Woods 1967: 133)
If people aren't meek when they inherit the earth, they will be when they get the mortgage paid off. (McKenzie 1980: 329)
It's just as well that the meek will inherit the earth; no one else would stand for the inheritance tax. (Esar 1968: 428)
"No, I didn't say the meek would inherit the earth. I think the meek are a pain in the neck." (*Punch*, April 25, 1979: 707)
So far it's been the other way around: the earth has inherited the meek. (Esar 1968: 359)
Some of us wonder how long the meek can keep the earth after they inherit it! (McKenzie 1980: 329)
The meek may inherit the earth, but it's the grumpy who get promoted. (Mingo and Javna 1989: 247)
The meek may inherit the earth, but they'll cease being meek as soon as they come into their inheritance. (Fuller 1943: 159)
The meek may inherit the earth just in time to see it sold for

200

taxes. (McKenzie 1980: 329)

The meek shall inherit the earth and the earth shall inherit holes in the ozone layer. (Liu and Vasselli 1996)

The meek shall inherit the earth, but they won't stay meek after they get it. (Esar 1968: 813)

The meek shall inherit the earth - they won't have the nerve to refuse. (Safian 1967: 13)

The meek shall inherit the earth
Why do they deserve such punishment? (Safian 1967: 19)

The meek will inherit the earth, but only after the courageous ones have taken off for the moon. (Esar 1968: 530)

The meek will probably be pushed off the earth long before they get a chance to inherit it. (Esar 1968: 428)

When the meek inherit the earth it's going to be lots of fun watching the unmeek take it away from them. (Woods 1967: 27)

When the time comes for the meek to inherit the earth, taxes will most likely be so high that they won't want it. (McKenzie 1980: 329)

The pen is mightier than the sword.
(DAP 457; ODEP 618; CODP 200; MPPS 480; NTC 206)
{The written word is more effective than physical force.}

A chicken coop is responsible for another famous proverb. It seems that a hen saw some choice corn beneath a board. The hen tugged and tugged until it got the board out of the way. A watching farmer casually remarked, "*The hen is mightier than the board.*" (Howard 1989: 257)

An editor is a man to whom the wastebasket is mightier than the pen. (Esar 1968: 256)

The pen is mightier than...the pencil. (Monteiro 1968: 128; Kandel 1976)

The pen is pointier than the sword. (Donald Elman, in Berman 1997: 320)

The penis is mightier than the sword. (Read 1978: 27; Rees 1981: 100)

The pension is mightier than the sword. (Anonymous 1908: 47)

"No, I didn't say the meek would inherit the earth.
I think the meek are a pain in the neck."

"And remember that the way to a man's heart
hangs just below his stomach."

The pun is mightier than the sword. (Loomis 1949: 356)

The proof of the pudding is in the eating.
(DAP 487; ODEP 650; CODP 208; MPPS 513; NTC 206-207)
{The wisdom of any action may be tested by putting it into practice.}
The proof is in the puffing. (Merit cigarettes advertisement). (*Working Woman*, May 1, 1989: 170)
The proof of the pudding is in the eating, and the proof of the marriage is in the cheating. (Esar 1968: 425)
The proof of the pudding is not in the eating, but in the digesting. (Esar 1968: 222)

The road to hell is paved with good intentions.
(DAP 297, 644, 514; ODEP 367; CODP 216; MPPS 673; NTC 207)
{Merely good intentions, not translated into actions, are of no value.}
Hell is paved with big pretensions. (*Cynic*, 1903, in Berman 1997: 187)
Hell is paved with good intentions - also asbestos. (Wurdz 1904)
The road to health is paved with food abstentions. (Safian 1967: 41)
The road to hell is always in good repair because its users pay so dearly for its upkeep. (Berman 1997: 187)
The road to hell is paved by the same contractors as all the other roads. (Weller 1982)
The road to hell is paved. It has to be; it gets a lot of traffic. (Berman 1997: 187)
The road to hell is paved with cheating evangelists. (Liu and Vasselli 1996)
The road to hell is paved with good conventions. (Berman 1997: 187)
The road to the patent office is paved with good inventions. (Berman 1997: 187)

The way to a man's heart is through his stomach.
(DAP 293; ODEP 871-872; CODP 272-273; MPPS 673; NTC
209-210)
{The best way of making a man love you is to feed him well.}
A woman who thinks the way to a man's heart is through his
stomach is aiming a little too high. (Kilroy 1985: 429)
A woman's way to a man's heart is through his stomach, but not
by jumping down his throat. (Esar 1968: 179)
"And remember that the way to a man's heart hangs just below
his stomach." (*Playboy*, May 1981: 248)
Any smart woman will tell you that the best way to a man's
heart is through his ego. (McKenzie 1980: 151)
Cosmetic Clerk: "You know what the fastest way to a man's
heart is?"
Roseanne: "Yeah. Through his chest!" (Mingo and Javna 1989:
20)
Girls often wear bathing suits with bare midriffs because the way
to a man's heart is through the stomach. (Esar 1968: 769)
The best way to a businessman's heart is through his stomach.
(*Punch*, July 15, 1988: 30-31)
The best way to a man's stomach...Nordic Track. (Nordic Track
exercising machine advertising). (*New Yorker*, March 4, 1991:
71)
The way to a man's heart is through his stomach, but a much
easier way is through flattery. (Esar 1968: 313)
The way to a man's pocketbook is through his stomach. (*St.
Louis Post-Dispatch*, February 4, 1975: 8D)
The way to a man's stomach is through his esophagus. (Weller
1982)
The way to a woman's heart is through his wallet. (Esar 1968:
851)
The way to a woman's heart is through the door of a good
restaurant. (Richard Needham, in Berman 1997: 186)
With Interwoven Jiffies, the quickest way to a man's heart is
through his feet. (Interwoven slippers advertisement). (*Woman's
Day*, December 13, 1977: 78)

There are more ways (than one) to kill [of killing] a cat (than choking her with cream).
[There's more than one way to skin a cat].
(DAP 87; ODEP 872; CODP 273; MPPS 670-671; NTC 214)
{You can find more than one way to achieve your purpose.}
There's more than one way to scan a cat! (*Bloomington Sunday Herald-Times*, October 25, 1981: without pages)
There's more than one way to skin a cabbage. (Anonymous 1961: 200)
There's more than one way to skin a cat – but not the same cat. (Esar 1968: 116)
There's more than one way to skin a Jap! (Felt & Tarrant Manufacturers advertisement). (*Fortune*, October 1942: 137)

There are other fish in the sea.
[There are better fish in the sea than have ever been caught; There are as good fish in the sea as ever came out of it].
(DAP 213; CODP 97; MPPS 228; NTC 210)
{Just because you have lost one good opportunity (usually a girlfriend or boyfriend), does not mean you will never find another.}
There are better fish stories in the sea than ever came out of it. (Esar 1968: 311)
There are plenty of fish in the sea...just make sure yours tests HIV negative. (Liu and Vasselli 1996)

There are two sides to every question.
(DAP 539-540; ODEP 852; CODP 264-265; MPPS 564; NTC 211)
{Most questions or situations have more than one answer.}
If there are two sides to every question, why is there only one answer? (McKenzie 1980: 436)
In prison there are two sides to every question - the inside and the outside. (Esar 1968: 632)
The bigot agrees there are two sides to every question - his side and the wrong one. (McKenzie 1980: 45)

There are two sides to every man: the side his wife knows, and the side he thinks she doesn't know. (Esar 1968: 403)
There are two sides to every political question, but only one office. (Esar 1968: 261)
There are two sides to every question, except when it happens to be a love triangle. (McKenzie 1980: 314)

There's a time and place for everything.
(DAP 597; CODP 255; MPPS 627; NTC 212)
{Everything has its appointed time or place to happen.}
To the mother of young children, there's a time and place for everything, except rest. (Esar 1968: 533)
Never slap a child in the face. Remember, there's a *place* for everything. (McKenzie 1980: 75)

There's always room at the top.
(DAP 515; CODP 218; MPPS 536-537)
{The proverb is used to encourage the average man to work hard.}
Cheer up! - there is always room at the bottom. (Hubbard 1973: 134)
Prices seem to think there is plenty of room at the top. (McKenzie 1980: 111)
There's always plenty of room at the top - for prices. (Esar 1968: 630)
There's always room at the top - after the investigation. (Oliver Herford, in Woods 1967: 493)
There's plenty of room at the top, but not enough for the people who think they ought to be there. (Esar 1968: 712)
There's plenty of room at the top, but not much company. (Esar 1968: 777)

There's many a slip 'twixt [between] (the) cup and (the) lip.
(DAP 546-547; ODEP 160; CODP 165; MPPS 575; NTC 214)
{Nothing is certain; things may go wrong while we are carrying out our plans.}

There is many a cup 'twixt the lip and the slip. (Edmund and Williams 1921: 147)

There's many a damn 'twixt the door and the jamb. (Esar 1968: 241)

There's many a slip 'twixt hiccup and lip. (Safian 1967: 41)

There's many a slip 'twixt the cup and the lip; the safest way is to drink out of the bottle. (Esar 1968: 91)

There's many a slip 'twixt the head and the pillow. (Loomis 1949: 356)

There's many a slip 'twixt the toe and the heel. (Wurdz 1904; Anonymous 1908: 56)

There's many a trip 'twixt the hip and the lip. (Loomis 1949: 356)

There's no accounting for tastes.
(DAP 5, 583; ODEP 2; CODP 1-2; MPPS 3; NTC 213)
{People differ in their tastes and preferences.}
There's no accounting for love: many a girl cannot put a man out of her mind even after he has put her out of his life. (Esar 1968: 22)

"There's no accounting for people's taste," said the cat as it licked its master's boots. (Mieder and Kingsbury 1994: 134)

There's no accounting for tastes...as the woman said when somebody told her her son was wanted by the police. (F. P. Adams, in Berman 1997: 400)

"There's no accounting for tastes," said the old maid as she kissed the cow. (Mieder and Kingsbury 1994: 135)

There's no fool like an old fool.
(DAP 225; ODEP 276; CODP 98-99; MPPS 237; NTC 215)
{If old people behave foolishly they are bigger fools than younger ones.}
Aesop, Jr.: "There's no *fuel* like an old *fuel!*"
Aesop, Sr.: "Hmmm....I *gas* you're right." (Mingo and Javna 1989: 197)

There is no fool like an old fool. Ask any young fool. (McKen-

zie 1980: 186)
There is no fool like the old fool who thinks he is fooling you.
(Esar 1968: 318; Prochnow 1988: 430)
There's no fool like an oiled fool. (Safian 1967: 41)
"There's no fool like an old fool," as the old man said when he
married his fourth wife. (Mieder and Kingsbury 1994: 49)
There's no fool like an old fool... but young fools combine
foolishness and ignorance in a way that can't be beat! (Berman
1997: 143)
There's no fool like an old fool, except an older fool. (Esar
1968: 318)
There's no fool like an old fool – you just can't beat experience.
(Esar 1968: 319)
There may be no fool like an old fool, but some members of our
young generation seem to be doing a pretty good job. (McKenzie
1980: 186)

There's no place like home.
[Be it ever so humble, there's no place like home].
(DAP 304; ODEP 629; CODP 202; MPPS 499; NTC 215)
{Home is the place where we feel happiest.}
Be it ever so homely, there's no face like your own. (Safian
1967: 35)
Be it ever so humble, there's no place like somewhere else.
(Esar 1968: 601)
Be it ever so humdrum, there's no place like home. (Esar 1968:
248)
Be it ever so mortgaged, there's no place like home. (Berman
1997: 192)
Be there ever so many payments, there's no place like home.
(Esar 1968: 532)
There is no place like home if you haven't got money to go out.
(McKenzie 1980: 240)
There is no place like home - where we are treated the best and
grumble the most. (McKenzie 1980: 222)
There's no place like Hilton. (Hilton Hotel advertisement). (*New*

Yorker, April 14, 1980: 93)

"There's no place like home," as the loafer said ven he crept under a market stall for a night's repose. (Mieder and Kingsbury 1994: 63)

There's no place like home, especially when your wife wants you to go with her to visit her relatives. (Esar 1968: 847)

There's no place like home - once in a while. (Metcalf 1993: 105)

There's no place like home – when you are not invited anywhere. (Esar 1968: 390)

There's no place like home - which is why I go out most nights. (Metcalf 1993: 105)

There's no place like home, which is why so many husbands go out nights. (Esar 1968: 389)

There's no place like Spiegel. (Spiegel catalogue advertisement). (*Better Homes & Gardens*, September 1979: 117)

There's no taste like home. (Del Monte menus advertisement). (*Co-Ed*, February 1979: 67)

There's no rest [peace] for the weary [wicked].
(DAP 506; MPPS 530; NTC 213)
{Even a tired, a worn-out person has to do more work.}
Rest Area: Not for the Wicked. (*New Yorker*, May 30, 1977: 84)
There is no rest for the wary. (Kandel 1976)
There may be no rest for the wicked, but there is often arrest. (Esar 1968: 276)

There's no such thing as a free lunch.
(CODP 101-102; NTC 216)
{You can't get anything for free.}
A business conference is a meeting in which everyone agrees that there is no such thing as a free lunch while eating one. (Berman 1997: 253)

There is no such thing as a calorie-free lunch. (Joan Beck, in Berman 1997: 253)

There's no such thing as a free lunch...but there is always free

210

cheese in a mousetrap. (Berman 1997: 253)

There's no time like the present.
(DAP 482, 598; ODEP 824; CODP 256; MPPS 626; NTC 216)
{The time to act is at once.}
I gave my wife a watch for her birthday. I figure there's no present like the time. (Henny Youngman, in Berman 1997)
There is no time like the pleasant. (Anonymous 1908: 35; Safian 1967: 38)
There is no time like the present for a present. (Esar 1952: 91)
There's no present like the *Times*. (*New York Times* advertisement). (*New York Times (Book Reviews)*, January 2, 1977: 24)
There's no time like the present for putting off things. (Esar 1968: 620)

There's nothing new under the sun.
(DAP 429; ODEP 580; CODP 186; MPPS 454-455; NTC 214)
{Even the very latest novelty has happened before.}
There is nothing new under the sun...but a joke is brand-new if you've never heard it before. (Berman 1997: 298)
There is nothing new under the sun or a harem skirt. (Hubbard 1973: 145)
There's nothing new under the nun. (Farman 1989)
There's nothing new under the sun, but on the beach there's a lot more of it showing. (Esar 1968: 67)
There's nothing new under the sun, but there are lots of old things we don't know. (Esar 1968: 410)

There's safety in numbers.
(DAP 522; ODEP 691; CODP 221; MPPS 544; NTC 214)
{Being surrounded by a group of people gives you a safer position.}
If you think there's safety in numbers, try playing roulette. (Esar 1968: 556)
There is safety in numbers...mused the student as he changed his major from philosophy to accounting. (Berman 1997: 364)

There's safety in numbers, but there's danger in figures. (Esar 1968: 307)

Think twice before you speak.
[Think first and speak afterwards. Think twice, speak once.]
(DAP 591; ODEP 263; CODP 252; MPPS 621)
{Think thoroughly before you start speaking.}
Diplomacy: thinking twice before saying nothing. (Berman 1997: 372)
Experience teaches wisdom: the experienced husband has learned to think twice before saying nothing. (Esar 1968: 286)
Think twice before you speak, and the other fellow will make the clever remarks first. (Esar 1968: 143)
Think twice before you speak and then talk to yourself. (Hubbard 1973: 97)
Think twice before you speak - especially to a friend in need. (Esar 1968: 809)

Those who can, do; those who can't, teach.
(DAP 81; CODP 35; MPPS 90; NTC 217-218)
{A stereotypical view of the inabilities of teachers.}
"It's like my mama always says, 'Those who can, do. Those who can't, talk about it so much you want to stuff a sofa cushion up their mouths.'" (Aileen Foster, in Mingo and Javna 1989: 133)
Those who can, do. Those who can't, attend conferences. (Berman 1997: 401)
Those who can - do. Those who can't - criticize. (McKenzie 1980: 6)
Those who can, do; those who can't, teach; and those who can't do anything at all, teach the teachers. (Braude 1955: 132)
Those who can, do - those who can't, teach - and those who can't teach, lecture on the sociology of education degrees. (Rees 1980: 126)
Those who can, do; those who can't, teach. And those who can't teach, teach teachers. (Feibleman 1978: 21)

212

Those who can't teach, administrate. Those who can't administrate, run for office. (Berman 1997: 401)
To say that those who can, do, and that those who can't, teach
is far from fair. (George Bernard Shaw, in Braude 1955: 132)

Time and tide wait for no man.
(DAP 598; ODEP 822; CODP 255; MPPS 628; NTC 218)
{Things will not wait for you, do not delay taking action.}
Time and tide take man for a ride. (Esar 1968: 333)
Time and tide wait for no man
But a woman expects all three to wait for her. (Safian 1967: 20)
Time and tide wait for no man - but a woman will. (McKenzie
1980: 558)
Time and tide wait for no man - But time always stands still for
a woman of thirty. (Wurdz 1904; Robert Frost, in McLellan
1996: 225)
Time, tide and bus drivers wait for no man. (Esar 1968: 103)
Time, tide and women drivers wait for no man. (Safian 1967:
37)
Time waits for no man, but it usually hesitates a while for a
woman of twenty-nine. (Esar 1968: 812)

Time flies.
(DAP 598; ODEP 823; CODP 255; MPPS 628; NTC 218)
{Time passes very quickly.}
"How time flies," as the monkey said when it threw the clock at
the missionary. (Mieder and Kingsbury 1994: 139)
No wonder time flies - there are so many people trying to kill it.
(Esar 1968: 812)
Since time flies, it's up to you to be the navigator. (McLellan
1996: 225)
Time flies
But for goldbrickers it just seems to be bucking head winds.
(Safian 1967: 24)

Time heals all wounds.
[Time is a [the] great healer].
(DAP 598; ODEP 823; CODP 256; MPPS 628; NTC 218-219)
{All insults, injuries and hurts heal over time.}
If you think time heals everything, try sitting in a doctor's office. (McKenzie 1980: 398)
Time heals all non-fatal wounds. (Weller 1982)
Time heals all things - except leaky faucets. (Esar 1968: 812)
Time heals all wounds...and daily routine keeps them bandaged. (Berman 1997: 461)
Time heals everything, but don't try sitting it out in a doctor's reception room. (Esar 1968: 199)
Time wounds all heels. (Anonymous 1961: 200)

Time is money.
(DAP 599; ODEP 823-824; CODP 256; MPPS 629; NTC 219)
{Time is as valuable as money.}
Both management and unions agree that time is money. They just can't agree on how much! (Metcalf 1993: 215)
Dime is money. (Margo 1982: 16)
If time is money, why is it that wealthy executives never seem to have a moment to spare? (Esar 1968: 105)
Time is money, and many people pay their debts with it. (Josh Billings, in Esar 1952: 203)
"Time is money," as the man said ven he stole the patent lever watch. (Mieder and Kingsbury 1994: 138)
Time is money, but not when you're doing it in jail. (Esar 1968: 632)
Time may be money, but it's much easier to persuade a man to give you his time than to lend you his money. (McKenzie 1980: 51)

To err is human (, to forgive divine).
(DAP 183; ODEP 225-226; CODP 79; NTC 220)
{All human beings are liable to commit sins and make mistakes.}
It's true that to err is human - but it can be overdone. (McKenzie

1980: 159)

Sign on a company bulletin board in Grand Rapids: "To err is human, to forgive is not company policy." (McKenzie 1980: 57)

To eat is human; to digest, divine. (Mark Twain, in Prochnow 1988: 342)

To err is humam. (Avis advertisement). (*Time*, October 22, 1973: 5)

To err is human, but it takes a computer to completely fuck things up. (Nierenberg 1994: 552)

To err is human
But only when we make the mistake. (Safian 1967: 25)

To err is human, but only when we ourselves make the mistake. (Esar 1968: 525)

To err is human, but to admit it isn't. (Safian 1967: 32; Esar 1968: 11)

To err is human, but to *really* screw things up you need a computer. (Metcalf 1993: 41)

To err is human - but usually a much better excuse is demanded. (Herbert V. Prochnow, Sr., in Prochnow 1988: 266)

To err is human, but when the eraser wears out before the pencil, you're overdoing it. (Esar 1968: 181)

To err is human; to blame it on someone else is even more human. (Esar 1968: 81)

To err is human; to cover it up is even more human. (McKenzie 1980: 159)

To err is human; to cover it up is, too. (Anonymous 1961: 200)

To err is human; to forget, routine. (McKenzie 1980: 159)

To err is human; to forgive is against university policy. (Haan and Hammerstrom 1980)

To err is human; to forgive, unusual. (Esar 1968: 324)

To err is human; to remain in error is stupid. (Prochnow 1988: 426)

To err is human - to totally muck things up needs a computer. (Kilroy 1985: 220)

To err is understandable; to admit it is unlikely. (McKenzie 1980: 101)

To err is humam.

That's why we invented the Wizard of Avis.

On one hand, nobody's perfect.
On the other hand, nobody cares to hear that when they're renting a car.
For instance, that rental agreement you get has 14 different trouble spots
on it where someone can easily make a mathematical error.
Add. Subtract. Multiply. Days. Hours. Discount. Mileage. Tax.
Why it's enough to drive a pretty young girl with a pen right up the wall.
Give her a break.
Rent from the pretty young girl in red.
She's the only one backed by the Wizard of Avis, a super-efficient computer
that neatly types out your entire rental agreement without making
mathematical errors.
(To get your free Wizard Number, simply visit your nearest Avis counter.
Or, call toll-free (800) 231-6900. In Texas, call (800) 392-3900.)
Just think: no more silly mistakes.

Avis rents all makes...features the Plymouth Fury.

© Avis Rent A Car System, Inc.

To err - is unlikely; to forgive - is unnecessary. (*New Yorker*, August 14, 1965: 24)

To itch is human, to scratch divine. (Berman 1997: 119)

To masturbate is human, to f..k, divine. (Yu and Jang 1975: 67)

To sleep is human. To sleep during the day is divine. (Edison advertisement). (*Newsweek*, December 7, 1981: 18A)

To speed is but human; to get caught, a fine. (Copeland 1965: 781; Safian 1967: 43)

You know what they say: to err is human, but it feels divine. (Metcalf 1993: 191)

Too many cooks spoil the broth.
(DAP 116; ODEP 831; CODP 258; MPPS 130-131; NTC 222)
{When too many people try to do the same thing at the same time, it is never done properly, and chaos reigns.}

Chefs make a meal of it.

But too many cooks spoil the brothel. (Kilroy 1985: 478)

Do too many chiefs spoil the military? (*New York Times*, January 20, 1985: 2E; Mieder 1989: 275)

Husband-seeking women

Too many looks spoil the troth. (Safian 1967: 30, 48)

In this house, only *one* cook spoils the broth. (*St. Louis Post-Dispatch*, November 29, 1975: 4B; Mieder 1993: 66)

The madam turned away oddballs and weirdos; too many kooks spoil the brothel. (Berman 1997: 67)

They say too many cooks spoil the broth... Gladys manages all by herself! (*Washington Post*, January 31, 1997: 1E)

Too many boys spoil the date. (Loomis 1949: 354)

Too many cooks clutter up the kitchen. (*The Burlington Free Press*, January 5, 1992: without pages)

Too many cooks spoil the figure. (Safian 1967: 30)

Too many legislators spoil reform. (Liu and Vasselli 1996)

Too much of a good thing (is worse than none at all).
(DAP 260; ODEP 831; CODP 258; MPPS 620; NTC 103)
{Nothing should be had in excess.}

Bigamy is the proof that there can be too much of a good thing. (Esar 1968: 76)

"Too much of a good thing," as the kitten said when she fell into the milk pail. (Mieder and Kingsbury 1994: 136)

Too much of a good thing can be wonderful. (Mae West, in Berman 1997: 280)

Travel broadens the mind.
(DAP 608; CODP 259; MPPS 641; NTC 222)
{Traveling teaches a lot.}

If travel broadens the mind, some people must be nailed to the ground. (Esar 1968: 519)

Travel broadens the mind...and loosens the bowels. (Berman 1997: 410)

Travel broadens the mind...and reduces the bank balance. (Berman 1997: 410)

Truth is stranger than fiction.
(DAP 617, 194; ODEP 844; CODP 88, 261; MPPS 648; NTC 82)
{Real life happenings are sometimes more bizarre than the wildest sensational stories people invent.}

Another thing stranger than fiction is woman. (Esar 1968: 879)

Ruth is stranger than fiction. (Kilroy 1985: 262)

The cold war is the truce that is stranger than fiction. (Esar 1968: 150)

To a liar, truth is more of a stranger than fiction. (Esar 1968: 472)

Truth is stranger than fiction, but never as popular. (Safian 1967: 12)

Truth is stranger than fiction, except science fiction. (Esar 1968: 828)

Truth is stranger than fiction - in lawsuits. (Safian 1967: 14)

Truth is stranger than fiction - to some people. (Mark Twain, in Prochnow 1988: 342)

Truth is stronger than fiction. (DAP 617)

Truth may be stranger than fiction, but fiction is truer. (Metcalf 1993: 218)
Youth is stranger than fiction. (Berman 1997: 420)

Two can live as cheap(ly) as one.
(DAP 620; MPPS 654)
{There are financial advantages for two people living together.}
A split personality is the only case where two can live as cheaply as one. (Esar 1968: 761)
Here's to economy, that enables two to live as cheaply as one thought he could. (Woods 1967: 287)
I suppose two can live as cheaply as one providing they both go out to work. (*Punch*, March 17, 1982: 421; Mieder 1989: 275)
If two can live as cheaply as one, it's because they have to. (McKenzie 1980: 110)
If two can live as cheaply as one - why don't they? (McKenzie 1980: 110)
In the good old days two could live as cheaply as one; nowadays one can live as expensively as two. (Esar 1968: 184)
Married folk have an advantage at Christmas. Two can give as cheaply as one. (Braude 1955: 240)
Newlyweds prove that two can live as cheaply as one – on parents. (Esar 1968: 548)
The only two who can live as cheaply as one are a dog and a flea. (Esar 1968: 239)
Two can live as cheap as one, but nowadays it takes both of them to earn enough to do it. (Herbert V. Prochnow, Sr., in Prochnow 1988: 270)
Two can live as cheaply as one, but it's worth the difference to stay single. (Esar 1968: 738)
Two can live as cheaply as one, but not so peacefully. (Esar 1968: 654)
Two can live as cheaply as one – but wives work because they don't care to live that cheap. (Safian 1967: 17)
Two can live as cheaply as one - for half as long. (Kilroy 1985: 201)

THE BORN LOSER ART SANSOM

"I suppose two can live as cheaply as one providing they both go out to work."

Two can live as cheaply as one – if both have good jobs. (Safian 1967: 17)
Two can live as cheaply as one – if one doesn't eat. (Esar 1968: 253)
Two can live as cheap as one if one's a horse and the other is a sparrow. (DAP 620)
"What do you say, sweetheart? Two can tread water as cheaply as one." (*New Yorker*, May 5, 1980: 35)
You know you've got inflation when one can live as cheaply as two. (Metcalf 1993: 118)

Two heads are better than one.
(DAP 288; ODEP 851; CODP 263-264; MPPS 297; NTC 222-223)
{Two people can solve a problem more easily than one.}
Four heads are better than one. (Frigidaire washers advertisement). (*McCall's*, August 1984: 11; Mieder 1989: 275)
Six heads are better than one. (Ronson shaver advertisement). (*Punch*, November 29, 1978: inside front cover)
Three heads are better than one (adjustment for inflation). (Liu and Vasselli 1996)
To the bigamist, two beds are better than one. (Esar 1968: 75)
Two dips are better than one. (Brach's chocolate advertisement). (*Family Circle*, November 15, 1983: 228; *Woman's Day*, December 13, 1983: 184)
"Two heads are better than one," as the cabbage-head said to the lawyer. (Mieder and Kingsbury 1994: 59)
Two heads are better than one - but not when they're soreheads. (Safian 1967: 17)
Two heads are better than one – except during a hangover. (Safian 1967: 17)
"Two heads are better than one," quoth the woman when she had her dog with her to the market. (Mieder and Kingsbury 1994: 59)
Two heads are better than one, unless you have a hangover. (Esar 1968: 367)

Two heads are not better than one, considering the present price of haircuts. (McKenzie 1980: 112)

Two is company, (but) three is a crowd [none].
(DAP 620-621; ODEP 851; CODP 264; MPPS 654-655; NTC 223)
{The presence of the third person is inconvenient, especially in the case of lovers or close friends who want to be by themselves.}
Before marriage, two's company and three's a crowd; after marriage, two's company and three's a great relief. (Esar 1968: 188)
Two is company, three is a crowd...and four is a bridge game. (Berman 1997: 63)
Two is company, three is an orgy. (Kandel 1976)
Two is company, three is poor birth control. (Safian 1967: 28)
Two is company, three is the result. (Safian 1967: 28; Metcalf 1993: 191)
Two is company, three's a crowd, four is a regiment, and five's not allowed. (DAP 620-621)
Two's company and three's a divorce. (Esar 1968: 237)
Two's company, three's a deformity. (Rees 1981: 101; Kilroy 1985: 354)
Two's company, three's a riot. (*Punch*, March 31, 1989: 14)
Two's company, three's great sex if you're kinky. (Liu and Vasselli 1996)
Two's company, three's...the muskateers. (Stark 1982)

Two wrongs don't make a right.
(DAP 683; ODEP 853; CODP 265; MPPS 706; NTC 223)
{An evil act can't be corrected with another evil act.}
Bigamy is the only crime on the books where two rites make a wrong. (McKenzie 1980: 45)
Bigamy is when two rites make a wrong. (Woods 1967: 300)
Two wrongs don't make a right...and three rights will get you back on the freeway. (Berman 1997: 463)

Two wrongs don't make a right, but they often make a fight. (Esar 1968: 307)
Two wrongs don't make a right, but two Wrights made an airplane. (Slung 1986: 83)

United we stand, divided we fall.
(DAP 625; CODP 266; MPPS 656; NTC 224)
{People who stick together are much harder to defeat than if they would be one by one.}
Divorced couples
United we stand, divided we can stand it better. (Safian 1967: 48)
"United we fall, divided we stand," as the temperance man said to the glass of liquor. (Mieder and Kingsbury 1994: 144)

Variety is the spice of life.
(DAP 630; ODEP 858; CODP 268; MPPS 658; NTC 225)
{Constant variation and change will make your life interesting and delightful.}
Bigamists
Variety is the spice of wife. (Safian 1967: 48)
Gossips are the spies of life. (Edmund and Williams 1921: 214)
Suicide is despise of life. (*Cynic*, 1905, in Berman 1997: 428)
Variety is the spice of collecting. (DAP 630)
Variety is the spice of Europe. (Europen Travel Commission advertisement). (*New Yorker*, February 24, 1962: 47)
"Variety is the spice of life," as the shoemaker said when he was chewing wax, leather, and tobacco, all at once. (Mieder and Kingsbury 1994: 145)
Variety is the spice of life, but for the suicide it's despise of life. (Safian 1967: 13)
Variety is the spice of love. (Condom advertisement). (*Oui*, March 1978: 119; *Ms.*, June 1979: 89; DAP 630)
You know what they say: variety is the life of spies. (Metcalf 1993: 73)

"So's vice."

VIRTUE IS ITS OWN REWARD

S.Kriggs

Virtue is its own reward.
(DAP 634; ODEP 861; CODP 269; MPPS 659; NTC 225)
{The reward for behaving virtuously is the satisfaction of having acted properly. So no one should expect any rewards for virtuous actions.}
Achievement has its own reward. (Corum watches advertisement). (*New York Times Magazine*, September 11, 1983: 3; Mieder 1989: 275)
Chastity is its own punishment. (Rees 1980: 37; Kilroy 1985: 383)
Money is its own reward. (Weller 1982)
On your birthday you should remember
that virtue is its own reward...
...But the other stuff has its compensations, too! (Hallmark greeting card purchased in February 1981 in Burlington, Vermont)
Ronald Reagan is his own reward. (Adler 1967: 41)
Sin is its own reward. (L.L. Levinson, in Berman 1997: 429)
Virtue is its own reward, and usually the only reward. (Esar 1968: 846)
Virtue is its own reward. So's vice. (*Playboy*, March 1977: 177)

Waste not, want not.
(DAP 641; ODEP 869; CODP 272; MPPS 664; NTC 226)
{If you do not waste anything, you will never be in need.}
Save not, have not. (U.S. Savings Bonds advertisement). (*Good Housekeeping*, May 1980: 281)
Waist not, want not. (*Better Homes & Gardens*, April 1977: 165; Mieder 1993: 68)

What can't be cured must be endured.
(DAP 131; ODEP 161; CODP 46; MPPS 144; NTC 227)
{If nothing can be done about a problem, you have to put up with it.}
What can't be cured must be insured. (Anonymous 1908: 19)
What can't be cured supports the doctor. (Esar 1968: 784)

WAIST NOT, WANT NOT.

Some things are not as they appear. Take a Dole banana. Sweet and plump and creamy enough to satisfy the hungries. Maybe you think it's loaded with calories. Uh-uh. A medium-size Dole banana contains only about 101 calories, no cholesterol and about as much fat as you'll find in lettuce. So when that 10 A.M. craving comes and you want to keep the scale tipped in your favor, grab a Dole banana. It's one snack that won't go to your waist.

**The Dōle Banana.
As a snack, it's a natural.**

What goes up must come down.
(DAP 626; CODP 266-267; NTC 227)
{Nothing remains on top forever.}
Food: what goes down must come up. (Mingo and Javna 1989: 79)
The fellow who said "What goes up must come down" must have lived before they invented taxes and postal rates. (McKenzie 1980: 498)
What goes up must come down...except the cost of living. (Berman 1997: 424)
What goes up must come down...only if it goes up with a velocity of less than 4.8 miles per second. (Berman 1997: 424)
What goes up must come down
Unless it orbits. (Safian 1967: 26)

What is sauce for the goose is sauce for the gander.
[What is sauce for the gander is sauce for the goose. What's good for the goose is good for the gander].
(DAP 524, 262; ODEP 699; CODP 222; MPPS 548; NTC 229)
{What is good for one person is good for another (very often about a man and a woman).}
This truth has been known from here to Menander: what's sauce for the gosling's not sauce for the gander. (James Thurber, *The Father and His Daughter*, in Thurber 1956: 53)
What is sauce for the goose may be sauce for the gander but it is not necessarily sauce for the chicken, the duck, the turkey, or the guinea hen. (Alice B. Toklas, in Berman 1997: 172)

What you don't know can't [doesn't; won't] hurt you.
(DAP 352-353; CODP 143; MPPS 356; NTC 228)
{Things unknown do not bother people.}
Censorship
The husband who doesn't tell his wife everything probably thinks that what she doesn't know won't hurt him. (Esar 1968: 410)
"Watergate or no Watergate...our motto is still 'What the public doesn't know can't hurt us'!" (*Time*, December 2, 1974: 98)

What a wife doesn't know doesn't hurt her, but it does give her friends something to talk about. (Esar 1968: 353)
What we don't know can't hurt us, but it can make us look pretty stupid at times. (DAP 352-353)
What you don't know can hurt you. (Metcalf 1993: 33)
What you don't know, doesn't hurt you, but it amuses a lot of people. (Esar 1968: 410)
"What you don't know doesn't hurt you" doesn't apply to the hidden taxes in the things you buy. (McKenzie 1980: 498)
What you don't know doesn't hurt you, except during an examination. (Esar 1968: 805)
What you don't know doesn't hurt you - unless you find out someone is getting paid for knowing what you don't. (McKenzie 1980: 286)
What you don't know won't hurt you - but it can make you look pretty stupid. (Safian 1967: 13)
What you don't know won't hurt you...so relax; you're invulnerable. (Berman 1997: 212)
What you don't know you can learn. (McKenzie 1980: 299)
What you don't owe won't hurt you. (Safian 1967: 41; Esar 1968: 418; McKenzie 1980: 125, Henny Youngman, in Berman 1997: 213)

When in doubt, do nowt [don't; do without; do nothing].
(DAP 166; ODEP 200; CODP 70; MPPS 184)
{Refrain from actions you are not sure about.}
As to the adjective, when in doubt, strike it out. (Mark Twain, in Esar 1968: 10)
When in doubt, be conventional. (Esar 1968: 241)
When in doubt, duck. (Malcolm Forbes, in Berman 1997: 106)
When in doubt, go home. (Esar 1968: 214)
When in doubt, let your horse do the thinkin'. (Alstad 1992: 111)
When in doubt, mind your own business. (Esar 1968: 241)
When in doubt, mumble. (Yu and Jang 1975: 157)
When in doubt, say no. (Slung 1986: 39; Berman 1997: 106)

When in doubt, tell the truth. (McKenzie 1980: 140)
When in doubt, worry. (Kilroy 1985: 28)
When in doubt, write a thank-you note. (Slung 1985: 5)

When in Rome, do as (the) Romans do.
(DAP 515; ODEP 683; CODP 217; MPPS 536; NTC 229-230)
{A visitor must follow the host's customs and ways of doing things, and must not expect the other people to change something just to please their guest.}
Most men when in Rome not only do as the Romans do, but see them, and go them one better. (Hubbard 1973: 169)
When in America, do as the French do. (Dubonnet advertisement). (*New Yorker*, December 24, 1979: 16)
When in Las Vegas, do as Caesar does. (Caesars Palace advertisement). (*San Diego Magazine*, July 1977: 35)
When in Rome do as the Romans do
Don't try it when the wife is along. (Safian 1967: 19)
When in Rome do as the Romans do?
My God! They don't do anything. (*Punch*, January 21, 1987: 25)
When in Rome do as the Romans do, that is, if the Romans do as they ought to do. (McKenzie 1980: 40)
When in Rome, just do it. (Liu and Vasselli 1996)

When poverty comes in at the door, love flies out of the window.
(DAP 390, 478; ODEP 642; CODP 205; MPPS 508; NTC 230)
{Love disappears when there is lack of money }
When grandparents enter the door, discipline flies out the window. (Esar 1968: 357)
When pa comes in at the door, ma's boyfriend flies out the window. (Berman 1997: 338)
When poverty comes in at the door, love should go out and get a job. (Esar 1968: 445)
When riches come in at the door, love flies around and bars all the exits. (Esar 1968: 684)

"Where there's a will there's a loophole!"

"When in Rome do as the Romans do?
My God! They don't do anything."

When the husband comes in at the door, the lover flies out of the window. (Ogden Nash, in Esar 1968: 14)
When the mother-in-law comes in at the door, love flies out of the window. (Safian 1967: 35; Berman 1997: 338)

When the going gets tough, the tough get going.
(CODP 111; NTC 231)
{At the time of adversity strong people take action and try harder.}
When the going gets tough, the smart get lost. (Robert Byrne, in Berman 1997: 409)
When the going gets tough, the tough get comfortable. (Lincoln advertisement). (*New Yorker*, July 15, 1996: 41)
When the going gets tough, the tough go shopping. (Berman 1997: 409)
When the going gets tough, the tough take a vacation. (Harry Browne, in Berman 1997: 409)
When the tough get going, they let sleeping dogs lie. (*The Burlington Free Press*, February 5, 1989: without pages)

Where ignorance is bliss, 'tis folly to be wise.
(DAP 325; ODEP 396; CODP 135; NTC 231)
{It is unwise to fight against stupidity or people you cannot change.}
When spinsterhood is bliss, 'tis folly to be wived. (Esar 1968: 760)
When spooning is bliss, 'tis folly to get married. (Loomis 1949: 355)
Where ignorance is bliss it's foolish to borrow your neighbor's newspaper. (Kin Hubbard, in Fuller 1943: 164)
Where ignorance is bliss, 'tis folly for a doctor to tell a patient what he has written on his prescription. (Esar 1968: 627)
Where ignorance is bliss, 'tis foolish to take an intelligence test. (Safian 1967: 29; Esar 1968: 434)
Where singleness is bliss 'tis folly to be married. (Copeland 1965: 782)

Where ignorance is bliss, 'tis folly to be wives. (Loomis 1949: 355)

Where there's a will, there's a way.
(DAP 655; ODEP 891; CODP 276; MPPS 683-684; NTC 231)
{If you truly want something, you can accomplish it in spite of obstacles.}
One old proverb originated differently than we hear it today. It seems that Bill was so much in love with May that he followed her wherever she went. People said, *Where there's a Bill, there's a May.* Someone twisted it around in later years to: *Where there's a will, there's a way.* (Howard 1989: 257)
Where's a will, there's a wail. (Rosten 1972: 34)
Where there's a bill, we're away. (Safian 1967: 44; Berman 1997: 441)
Where there's a pill, there's a way. (Kilroy 1985: 264)
Where there's a swill there's a sway. (Safian 1967: 41)
"Where there's a swill there's a way," as the hog said when he rooted the back gate off its hinges to come at the kitchen swill barrel. (Mieder and Kingsbury 1994: 132)
Where there's a will, there are dissatisfied relatives. (Esar 1968: 870)
Where there's a will - there's a contestant. (Safian 1967: 33)
Where there's a will - there's a delay. (Safian 1967: 33)
Where there's a will - there's a dissatisfied relative. (Safian 1967: 33)
Where there's a will - there's a greedy solicitor getting in on the act. (Kilroy 1985: 205)
Where there's a will, there's a lawsuit. (Wurdz 1904; Anonymous 1908: 26; Metcalf 1993: 227)
Where there's a will there's a lawyer's bill. (Safian 1967: 33)
Where there's a will there's a loophole! (*Punch*, June 14, 1978: 1017)
Where there's a will there's a wait. (Safian 1967: 44; *Vogue*, April 1978: 166)
Where there's a will, there's a way; but where there are many

wills, there's no way. (Esar 1968: 856)
Where there's a will there's a way out of it. (Loomis 1949: 357)
Where there's a will, there's a why. (Esar 1968: 870)
Where there's a will there's a won't. (Bierce 1958: 120; Barbour 1963: 100; *St. Louis Post-Dispatch*, August 8, 1974: 12D; Weller 1982)
Where there's a will, there's an inheritance tax. (Kandel 1976)
Where there's a will, you can expect a dead person's long-lost relatives to come out of the woodwork. (Liu and Vasselli 1996)
Where there's a Wills there's a way. (Wills World of Travel advertisement). (pamphlet from 1983)
Where there's a woman, there's a way - and she usually gets it. (Esar 1968: 856)
Where there's a won't, there's a way. (Esar 1968: 668)
Where there's a word there's a way. (*New York Times* advertisement). (*New Yorker*, January 19, 1957: 41)
You know what they say: where there's a will, there's relatives. (Metcalf 1993: 227)

Where [While] there's life, there's hope.
(DAP 375; ODEP 462; CODP 150; MPPS 372-373; NTC 232)
{People hope for improvements as long as they live.}
A small boy's lament: "While there's life, there's soap." (McKenzie 1980: 52)
"Ah well," said the painter, preparing a fresh canvas, "while there's still life there's hope." (Mieder and Kingsbury 1994: 127)
Spinsters
Where there's hope, there's life. (Safian 1967: 47; Esar 1968: 759)
Where there's life insurance, there's hope. (Esar 1968: 478)

Where there's smoke, there is fire.
(DAP 549; ODEP 573; CODP 232-233; MPPS 576; NTC 215)
{There is a cause and effect in all things.}

Where there's smoke there's controversy.

The papers are filled with stories against smoking.

But many people are continuing to smoke. They like it.

Yet it's obvious that there are smokers who have become concerned about what they've been hearing about 'tar' and nicotine. And so – many of them are trying lower 'tar' and nicotine cigarettes.

If you're a smoker who's become concerned, you (and millions like you) have been facing a dilemma.

Until Vantage, cigarettes that had lots of flavor had lots of 'tar' and nicotine. And cigarettes that were way down in 'tar' and nicotine were way down in taste.

Most smokers found that most low 'tar' cigarettes just didn't make it. But then we started making Vantage.

Vantage is not the lowest 'tar' and nicotine cigarette you'll find, but it could well be the lowest you'll enjoy. Exactly the right blend of tobacco working in harmony with the ingenious Vantage filter is what made it possible.

And that's why Vantage has become the fastest growing major cigarette brand in America.

There's no controversy about that.

VANTAGE
MENTHOL

VANTAGE
MENTHOL

MENTHOL 11 mg. tar
0.8 mg. nicotine

VANTAGE

FILTER 11 mg. tar
0.7 mg. nicotine

VANTAGE

Filter: 11 mg. "tar", 0.7 mg. nicotine, Menthol: 11 mg. "tar", 0.8 mg. nicotine, av. per cigarette, FTC Report OCT. '74.

The person who says, „Where there's smoke, there's fire," never owned a fireplace. (Esar 1968: 310)
Where there's smoke, there's burnt toast. (Berman 1997: 378)
Where there's smoke there's controversy. (Vantage cigarettes advertisement). (*Playboy*, May 1975: 45)
Where there's smoke there's fire, except when it's a cookout. (Esar 1968: 180)
Where there's smoke, there's flavor. (Old Smokehouse Bar-B-Q advertisement). (*Family Circle*, September 11, 1984: 205)
Where there's smoke there's pollution. (Weller 1982)
Where there's smoke, there's toast. (Metcalf 1993: 44)
Where there's smoking, there's cancer, heart disease, and emphysema. (Berman 1997: 378)
Where there's SUN, there's energy. (SUN Energy Company advertisement). (*US News & World Report*, August 5, 1985: without pages)

Who does not love wine, women and song, will remain a fool his whole life long.
(not registered in standard proverb dictionaries; but see Mieder 1983)
{People should enjoy life.}
Advice to the exhausted: When wine, women and song become too much for you, give up singing. (Adams 1969: 331)
It used to be wine, women and song. Now it's beer, the old lady, and TV. (T-shirt slogan located in September 1989 in Columbia, South Carolina; Berman 1997: 452)
When his doctor orders a playboy to cut out wine, women and song, the first thing he cuts out is singing. (Esar 1968: 234)

You are never too old to learn.
(DAP 438; ODEP 563; CODP 181)
{People of all age groups can learn new things.}
The man who is too old to learn today was the child who was too young to learn yesterday. (Esar 1968: 467)
The man who says he's too old to learn new things probably

always was. (McKenzie 1980: 299)

You are never too old to learn - to make new mistakes. (Esar 1968: 467)

You are never too old to learn, unless you're a teenager. (Esar 1968: 798)

You're never too old to do goody stuff. (Mingo and Javna 1989: 9)

You're never too old to learn
And what you learn makes you old. (Safian 1967: 19)

You're never too old to learn - some new way to be foolish. (Safian 1967: 15)

You're never too old to learn something stupid. (Berman 1997: 310)

You're never too old to yearn. (Berman 1997: 220)

You are only young once.
(DAP 686; MPPS 708)
{Youth cannot be repeated, so enjoy it while it lasts.}
We are only young once. This is all society can stand. (McKenzie 1980: 43)

You are only young once; after that you have to blame your mistakes on something else. (Esar 1968: 82)

You are what you eat.
(DAP 175; CODP 74)
{Our eating habits might be reflections on our character.}
"If we are what we eat, I don't want to be a cauliflower." (*The Burlington Free Press*, June 1, 1992: 4D)

"If we are what we eat, I'd rather not be a lima bean." (*Better Homes & Gardens*, March 1979: 230)

"Margaret says we are what we eat, and I don't want to be a carrot." (*The Burlington Free Press*, October 2, 1998: 4C)

Scientists tell us we are what we eat. Nuts must be more common in diets than we thought. (McKenzie 1980: 130)

We are what we eat
Nuts must be a part of lots of diets, it seems. (Safian 1967: 22)

THE FAMILY CIRCUS

"If we are what we eat, I don't
want to be a cauliflower."

Tony Auth

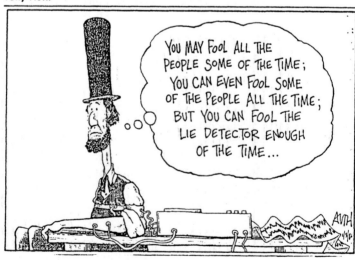

"You are what you drink, and I drink only the best." (*New Yorker*, September 2, 1985: 59)

You are what you eat...maybe, and you are how you eat, for sure. (Berman 1997: 112)

You are what you eat. That's why I called you a prick! (*Gallery*, April 1979: 14)

You are what you wear. (*Punch*, April 7, 1976: cover)

You are what you wheat. (Kretschmer Wheat Germ advertisement). (*Nation's Business*, November 1981: 27)

You are where you eat. (*New Yorker*, August 12, 1991: 53)

You can catch more flies with honey than vinegar.
[Honey catches more flies than vinegar.]
(DAP 217; CODP 129; MPPS 234; NTC 234)
{Kind and polite words can bring more success than demands or force.}

You can catch more flies with honey than vinegar...Keep that in mind next time you want a swarm of flies. (Berman 1997: 140)

You'll catch more flies with honey than you care to. (Weller 1982)

You can fool some of the people all the time, all the people some of the time, but you can't fool all the people all the time.
(DAP 460)
{Misleading people has its limits.}

A clever politician knows that it isn't necessary to fool all the people all the time – just during the campaign. (Esar 1968: 110)

A flirt fools some of the men all of the time, and all of the men some of the time, but not all of the men all of the time. (Esar 1968: 314)

Fooling some of the people some of the time is good enough for me. (*New Yorker*, February 16, 1976: 47)

Offer Rémy to all of your friends some of the time, some of your friends all of the time, but never all of your friends all of the time. (Rémy Martin advertisement). (*Punch*, September 29,

1982: 492a-b)

This survey indicates you can fool seventeen per cent of the people a hundred per cent of the time, thirty-four per cent of the people fifty-one per cent of the time, and a hundred per cent of the people twelve per cent of the time. (*New Yorker*, September 19, 1977: 43)

You can fool all of the people some of the time, and some of the people all of the time, and the rest of the time someone else will fool them. (Safian 1967: 16)

You can fool all of the people some of the time, but the rest of the time they will have to make fools of themselves. (Berman 1997: 144)

You can fool all of the people some of the time; you can fool some of the people all of the time; and that should be sufficient for most purposes. (Weller 1982)

You can fool all the people some of the time, but you can fool yourself all the time. (Herbert V. Prochnow, Sr., in Prochnow 1988: 268)

You can fool some of the people all of the time and all of the people some of the time, a combination of which keeps this company going! (Kilroy 1985: 129)

You can fool some of the people all of the time, and all of the people some of the time, but the rest of the time they will fool themselves. (Esar 1968: 711)

You can fool some of the people all of the time, and all of the people some of the time, but you can make a fool of yourself anytime. (Kandel 1976)

You can fool some of the people some of the time, but not your private secretary. (Esar 1968: 708)

You can fool too many of the people too much of the time. (James Thurber, *The Owl Who Was God*, in Thurber 1940: 36)

You can only fool some of the people some of the time because the rest of the time they are trying to fool you. (Esar 1968: 208)

You can't fool all of the people all of the time - but it isn't necessary. (Fuller 1943: 80)

You can't fool all the people all of the time, but the average

politician is contented with a sizable majority. (Copeland 1965: 786)
You can't fool all the people all the time
But lots of folks are always trying. (Safian 1967: 22)
You can't fool all the people all the time, but politicans figure that once every four years is good enough. (McKenzie 1980: 154)
You may fool all the people some of the time; you can even fool some of the people all of the time; but you can fool the lie detector enough of the time. (*The Burlington Free Press*, January 12, 1986: 12A)

You can lead a horse to (the) water, but you can't make him drink.
(DAP 312-313; ODEP 449; CODP 131; MPPS 322; NTC 234)
{You can present people with an opportunity but you can't force them to act.}
You can educate a fool but you can't make him think. (Alstad 1992: 36)
You can elect the President to the White House, but you can't make him think. (Liu and Vasselli 1996)
You can lead a crowd to culture, but you can't make 'em think!
(*New Yorker*, April 23, 1960: 71)
You can lead a fool to college, but you can't make him think. (Barbour 1963: 99)
You can lead a fraternity man to water, but why disappoint him. (Loomis 1949: 355)
You can lead a horse to water, but remember how a wet horse smells. (Berman 1997: 195)
You can lead a horse to water, but you can't make him walk on it! (*The Burlington Free Press*, September 23, 1994): 5D)
You can lead a horse to water but you can't make him water-ski. (*Standard Examiner*, June 14, 1995: 7B)
You can lead a man to Congress but you can't make him think. (McKenzie 1980: 104)
You can lead your boy to college but you can't make him think.

THE FAR SIDE

MOTHER GOOSE & GRIMM By MIKE PETERS

(Safian 1967: 36)
You may lead an ass to knowledge, but you cannot make him
think. (Anonymous 1908: 35)

You can't have [eat] your cake and eat [have] it (too).
(DAP 79; ODEP 215; CODP 124-125; MPPS 88; NTC 235)
{One can't pursue two alternatives or benefit from two incompat-
ible things, plans or actions at the same time.}
Beware of the girl who likes to eat her cake and have yours too.
(Esar 1968: 107)
You can't have your cake and eat it too...but you can't eat cake
unless you have it. (Berman 1997: 44)
You can't have your cake and eat it too...unless you bake two
cakes. (Berman 1997: 44)
You can't have your snake and beat it. (Farman 1989)

You can't judge [tell] a book by its cover.
(DAP 62; CODP 27; MPPS 65; NTC 71)
{Don't judge the value of something just from the way it looks.}
If you don't judge a book by its cover, why pay for the cover?
(Quality Paperback Book Club advertisement). (*New Yorker*,
October 17, 1977: 196)
Never judge a resort by its postcards. (Esar 1968: 677; McLellan
1996: 123)
You can't judge a book by its author. (Kandel 1976)
You can't judge a kiwifruit by its cover. (Kiwifruit adver-
tisement). (*Woman's Day*, January 8, 1985: 123; *Good House-
keeping*, November 1985: 298)
You can't judge an egg by its cover. (Safeway Foods advertise-
ment). (*Family Circle*, June 19, 1984: 174; Mieder 1989: 275)
You can't tell a book by its movie. (Safian 1967: 35)
You can't tell a rook by its cover. (Farman 1989)

You can't keep a good man down.
(DAP 166; MPPS 399)
{A decent person will prevail.}

You can't judge an egg by its cover.

You have to look inside. So we do.
It's called Candling. And simply put, it involves passing the egg over a very bright light to determine that the yolk, and the white, are clear and intact.

Candling is just one of the things we do to make sure you get a good egg: one that you're expecting.

We weigh and grade them. We carefully clean them. We inspect them to make sure they're perfectly packed. (Store them in your refrigerator large end up; they'll stay fresher, longer.)

And then we rush them to our stores. So when you buy eggs at Safeway, you'll get a dozen good

fresh eggs, with not a bad one in the bunch. Or we'll pay for it.

We're a little particular about our eggs. But then we're a little particular about everything we sell.

We have to be.

We're Safeway, America's favorite food store... and we're proud to be part of your life.

SAFEWAY **AMERICA'S FAVORITE FOOD STORE.**

Jonah proved that you can't keep a good man down. (Esar 1968: 447)
You can't keep a good golfer downtown. (Copeland 1965: 792; Safian 1967: 38)
"You can't keep a good man down," as the lion said when he coughed up the Hebrew martyr. (Mieder and Kingsbury 1994: 36)
You can't keep a good man good. (Esar 1968: 351)

You can't make a silk purse out of a sow's ear.
(DAP 491; ODEP 733; CODP 230; MPPS 515-516; NTC 235-236)
{You can't make something excellent out of poor materials, neither can you change a person's real character.}
You can't make a silk purse out of a sow's ear, but a smart gal knows how to get a mink out of an old goat. (Safian 1967: 14)
You can't make a silk purse out of a sow's ear...or a sow's ear out of a silk purse. (Berman 1997: 347)
You can't make a silk purse out of polyestor. (*The Burlington Free Press*, June 3, 1995: 1C)

You can't teach an old dog new tricks.
(DAP 162; ODEP 805; CODP 250; MPPS 179; NTC 237)
{People who are used to doing things in a particular way do not welcome any innovations or changes. They might even be incapable of change.}
"Well, if ya can't teach an old dog new tricks, maybe you should get a new dog!" (*The Burlington Free Press*, January 3, 1991: without pages)
You can't teach an old dog new tricks...but old fleas don't mind a new dog. (Berman 1997: 102)
You can't teach an old dog new tricks, but you can use him as a doorstop. (Liu and Vasselli 1996)
You can't teach an old dog new tricks...so long as his old tricks keep working. (Seth Haven, in Berman 1997: 102)

"Just remember – two's company, three's a riot."

DENNIS, THE MENACE

"WELL, IF YA CAN'T TEACH AN OLD DOG NEW TRICKS, MAYBE YOU SHOULD GET A *NEW DOG!*"

You don't get something for nothing.
(DAP 551; CODP 234; MPPS 582; NTC 237-238)
{You have to pay for everything in life.}
Things always balance out: when someone gets something for nothing, someone else gets nothing for something. (Esar 1968: 255)
You cannot get something for nothing - unless it's a weed. (Esar 1968: 861)

You never miss the water till the well runs dry.
(DAP 642-643; ODEP 435; CODP 171; MPPS 666; NTC 239)
{People don't value what they have until they lose it.}
We never miss the waiter till our throats go dry. (Berman 1997: 437)
You will never miss water until the champagne runs dry. (Anonymous 1908: 76)

246

Bibliography

References:

References to several Anglo-American proverb collections have been provided using the following abbreviations followed by the page numbers:

DAP   Mieder, Wolfgang, Stewart A. Kingsbury and Kelsie B. Harder (eds.) (1992). *A Dictionary of American Proverbs*. New York: Oxford University Press.

ODEP   Wilson, F.P. (1970). *The Oxford Dictionary of English Proverbs*. 3rd ed. Oxford: Oxford University Press (1st ed. 1935 by William George Smith).

CODP   Simpson, John A. (1993) *The Concise Oxford Dictionary of Proverbs*. 3rd ed. Oxford: Oxford University Press.

MPPS   Whiting, Barlett Jere. (1989). *Modern Proverbs and Proverbial Sayings*. Cambridge, Massachusetts: Harvard University Press.

NTC   Bertram, Anne (1994). *NTC's Dictionary of Proverbs and Clichés*. Lincolnwood, Illinois: National Textbook Company.

Sources:

Additional sources, especially advertisements, caricatures, cartoons, and comic strips, are cited with complete bibliographical information from Wolfgang Mieder's international proverb archive in Burlington, Vermont (USA). Almost every book listed here is also part of this archive.

Abel, Bob (ed.) (1974). *The American Cartoon Album*. New York: Dodd, Mead & Company. (without pages).

Adams, A. K. (1969). *The Home Book of Humorous Quotations*.

New York: Dodd, Mead & Company.

Adams, Joey (1959). *It Takes One to Know One*. New York: G.P. Putnam's Sons.

Adler, Bill (1967). *Bill Adler's Graffiti*. New York: Pyramid Books.

Alstad, Ken (1992). *Savvy Sayin's*. 10th printing. Tucson, Arisona: Ken Alstad Company (first published in 1986).

Anonymous (1908). *Toasts and Maxims. A Book of Humour to Pass the Time*. New York R.F. Fenno & Company.

Anonymous (1961). Perverted Proverbs. *Western Folklore* 20, 200.

Anonymous (1965). Parodied Proverbs from Idaho. *Western Folklore* 24, 289-290.

Anonymous (1982). *Mother Tried to Tell Me...and I Just Wouldn't Listen*. New York: Periwinkle Inc.

Barber, John W. (1858). *The Hand Book of Illustrated Proverbs*. New York: George F. Tuttle.

Barbour, Frances M. (1963). Some Uncommon Sources of Proverbs. *Midwest Folklore* 13, 97-100.

Barbour, Frances M. (1964). Embellishment of the Proverb. *Southern Folklore Quarterly* 27, 291-298.

Bauman, Richard, and Neil McCabe (1970). Proverbs in an LSD Cult. *Journal of American Folklore* 83, 318-324.

Berman, Lous A. (1997). *Proverb Wit & Wisdom: A Treasury of Proverbs, Parodies, Quips, Quotes, Clichés, Catchwords, Epigrams and Aphorisms*. Berkeley, California: A Perigee Book.

Bertram, Anne (1994). *NTC's Dictionary of Proverbs and Clichés*. Lincolnwood, Illinois: National Textbook Company.

Bierce, Ambrose (1958). *The Devil's Dictionary*. New York: Dover Publications (Bierce compiled this work between 1881 and 1906).

Braude, Jacob M. (1955). *Speaker's Encyclopedia of Stories, Quotations and Anecdotes*. New York: Prentice-Hall, Inc.

Bronner, Simon J. (1982). The Haptic Experience of Culture

248

["Seeing is Believing, but Feeling is the Truth"]. *Anthropos* 77, 351-362.

Carnes, Pack (1986). The American Face of Aesop: Thurber's Fables and Tradition. *Moderna Språk* 79, 3-17. Also in P. Carnes (ed.), *Proverbia in Fabula: Essays on the Relationship of the Fable and the Proverb*. Bern: Peter Lang, 1988. 311-331.

Colombo, John Robert (1975). *Little Book of Canadian Proverbs, Graffiti, Limericks, and other Vital Matters*. Edmonton, Alberta: Hurtig Publishers.

Copeland, Lewis and Faye (1965). *10,000 Jokes, Toasts and Stories*. New York: Doubleday.

Doyle, Charles Clay (1996). On "New" Proverbs and the Conservativeness of Proverb Dictionaries. *Proverbium* 13, 69-84.

Dundes, Alan (1966). Here I Sit: A Study of American Latrinalia. *The Kroeber Anthropological Society Papers*, no. 34, 91-105.

Dundes, Alan (1966). Metafolklore and Oral Literary Criticism. *The Monist* 50, 505-516.

Dundes, Alan (1972). Seeing is Believing. *Natural History*, no. 5, 8-14 and 86. Also in A. Dundes, *Interpreting Folklore*. Bloomington, Indiana: Indiana University Press, 1980. 86-92.

Edmund, Peggy, and Harold Workman Williams (1921). *Toaster's Handbook: Jokes, Stories and Quotations*. New York: The H.W. Wilson Company.

Esar, Evan (1945). *Esar's Joke Dictionary*. New York: Harvest House Publishers.

Esar, Evan (1952). *The Humor of Humor*. New York: Horizon Press.

Esar, Evan (1968). *20,000 Quips and Quotes*. Garden City, New York: Doubleday & Company.

Farman, John (1989). *You Can't Tell a Rook by Its Cover*. London: Pan Books Ltd. (without pages).

Feibleman, James K. (1978). *New Proverbs for Our Day*. New

York: Horizon Press.

Flavel, Linda and Roger (1994). *Dictionary of Proverbs and Their Origins*. London: Kyle Cathie Ltd. (first published in 1993).

Flexner, Stuart, and Doris Flexner (1993). *Wise Words and Wives' Tales*. New York: Avon Books.

Fuller, Edmund (1943). *Thesaurus of Epigrams*. New York: Crown Publishers.

Haan, Marina N., and Richard B. Hammerstrom (1980). *Graffiti in the Big Ten*. Madison, Wisconsin: Brown House Galleries. (without pages).

Howard, Vernon (1989). Our Famous Proverbs. In Wolfgang Mieder (1989): 256-257 (first published in V. Howard, *Humorous Monologues*. New York: Sterling Publishing Co., 1955. 109-110).

Hubbard, Elbert (1973). *A Thousand & One Epigrams*. New Jersey: Prentice-Hall, Inc.

Kandel, Howard (1976). *The Power of Positive Pessimism: Proverbs for Our Time*. 9th printing. Los Angeles: Price, Stern, Sloan Publishers. (without pages).

Kehl, D.G. (1977). Roman Hands Gave Us the Verbal Finger. *Maledicta* 1, 283-292.

Keyes, Ralph (1992). *"Nice Guys Finish Seventh": False Phrases, Spurious Sayings, and Familiar Misquotations*. New York: HarperCollins Publishers.

Kilroy, Roger (1985). *Graffiti: The Scrawl of the Wild and Other Tales from the Wall*. London: Gorgi Books.

Lau, Kimberly J. (1996). "It's about Time": The Ten Proverbs Most Frequently Used in Newspapers and Their Relation to American Values. *Proverbium: Yearbook of International Proverb Scholarship* 13, 135-159.

Legman, Gershon (1968). *Rationale of the Dirty Joke: An Analysis of Sexual Humor*. New York: Bell Publishing Company.

Liu, Paul, and Robert Vasselli (1996). *Proverbial Twists*. Highland Park, New Jersey: Johanne Inc. (without pages).

Lobel, Arnold (1980). *Fables*. New York: HarperCollins Publishers.

Loomis, C. Grant (1949). Traditional American Wordplay: The Epigram and Perverted Proverbs. *Western Folklore* 8, 348-357.

Margo, Egdon H. (1982). Missqprints [*sic*]. *Verbatum: The Language Quartely*, no. 3, 16.

Massing, Jean Michel (1995). From Greek Proverb to Soap Advert [*sic*]: Washing the Ethiopian. *Journal of the Wartburg and Courtauld Institutes* 58, 180-201.

McKenzie, Alyce M. (1996). "Different Strokes for Different Folks": America's Quintessential Postmodern Proverb. *Theology Today* 53, 201-212.

McKenzie, E.C. (1980). *Mac's Giant Book of Quips & Quotes*. Grand Rapids, Michigan: Baker Book House.

McLellan, Vern (1996). The Complete Book of Practical Proverbs & Wacky Wit. Wheaton, Illinois: Tyndale House Publishers.

Metcalf, Fred (1993). *The Penguin Dictionary of Jokes, Wisecracks, Quips and Quotes*. New York: Viking.

Mieder, Wolfgang (1978). Proverbial Slogans Are the Name of the Game. *Kentucky Folklore Record* 24, 49-53.

Mieder, Wolfgang (1981). The Proverbial Three Wise Monkeys. *Midwestern Journal of Language and Folklore* 7, 5-38.

Mieder, Wolfgang (1982/85/89). *Antisprichwörter*. 3 vols. Wiesbaden: Verlag für deutsche Sprache. Wiesbaden: Gesellschaft für deutsche Sprache. Wiesbaden: Quelle & Meyer.

Mieder, Wolfgang (1983). "Wine, Women and Song": From Martin Luther to American T-Shirts. *Kentucky Folklore Record* 29, 89-101.

Mieder, Wolfgang (1985). A Proverb a Day Keeps no Chauvinism Away. *Proverbium: Yearbook of International Proverb Scholarship* 2, 273-277.

Mieder, Wolfgang (1987). *Tradition and Innovation in Folk Literature*. Hanover, New Hampshire: University Press of New England.

Mieder, Wolfgang (1989). *American Proverbs: A Study of Texts and Contexts*. Bern: Peter Lang.

Mieder, Wolfgang (1990). "A Picture Is Worth a Thousand Words": From Advertising Slogan to American Proverb. *Southern Folklore* 47, 207-225.

Mieder, Wolfgang (1991). "An Apple a Day Keeps the Doctor Away": Traditional and Modern Aspects of English Medical Proverbs. *Proverbium: Yearbook of International Proverb Scholarship* 8, 77-106.

Mieder, Wolfgang (1993). *Proverbs Are Never Out of Season: Popular Wisdom in the Modern Age*. New York: Oxford University Press.

Mieder, Wolfgang (1993). "The Grass Is Always Greener on the Other Side of the Fence": An American Proverb of Discontent. *Proverbium: Yearbook of International Proverb Scholarship* 10, 151-184.

Mieder, Wolfgang (1994). *Wise Words: Essays on the Proverb*. New York: Garland Publishing.

Mieder, Wolfgang (1997). *The Politics of Proverbs: From Traditional Wisdom to Proverbial Stereotypes*. Madison, Wisconsin: The University of Wisconsin Press.

Mieder, Wolfgang (1998). *Verdrehte Weisheiten: Antisprichwörter aus Literatur und Medien*. Heidelberg: Quelle & Meyer.

Mieder, Wolfgang, and Alan Dundes (1981). *The Wisdom of Many: Essays on the Proverb*. New York: Garland Publishing. Rpt. Madison, Wisconsin: The University of Wisconsin Press, 1994.

Mieder, Wolfgang, and Stewart A. Kingsbury (eds.) (1994). *A Dictionary of Wellerisms*. New York: Oxford University Press.

Mieder, Wolfgang, Stewart A. Kingsbury and Kelsie B. Harder (eds.) (1992). *A Dictionary of American Proverbs*. New York: Oxford University Press.

Militz, Hans-Manfred (1991). Das Antisprichwort als semantische Variante eines sprichwörtlichen Textes. *Proverbium: Yearbook of International Proverb Scholarship* 8, 107-111.

Mingo, Jack, and John Javna (1989). *Primetime Proverbs: The Book of TV Quotes*. New York: Harmony Books.

Monteiro, George (1968). Proverbs in the Re-Making. *Western Folklore* 27, 128.

Muller, Helen M. (1932). *Still More Toasts: Jokes, Stories and Quotations*. New York: The T.W. Wilson Company.

Myers, Robert (1968). *The Spice of Love: Wisdom and Wit About Love Through the Ages*. Kansas City, Missouri: Hallmark Cards, Inc.

Nierenberg, Jess (1994). Proverbs in Graffiti: Taunting Traditional Wisdom. In Wolfgang Mieder (ed.), *Wise Words: Essays on the Proverb*. New York: Garland Publishing, 543-561 (first published in *Maledicta* 7 [1983], 41-58).

Prochnow, Herbert V., and Herbert V. Prochnow, Jr. (1988). *The Toastmaster's Treasure Chest*. New York: Harper & Row Publishers.

Read, Allen Walker (1977). *Classic American Graffiti*. Waukesha, Wisconsin: Maledicta Press. (1st edition Paris: Privately Printed, 1935).

Read, Allen Walker (1978). Graffiti as a Field of Folklore. *Maledicta* 2, 15-31.

Rees, Ennis (1965). *Pun Fun*, New York: Abelard-Schuman.

Rees, Nigel (1979). *Graffiti Lives, OK*. London: Unwin Paperbacks.

Rees, Nigel (1980). *Graffiti 2*. London: Unwin Paperbacks.

Rees, Nigel (1981). *Graffiti 3*. London: Unwin Paperbacks.

Rees, Nigel (1991). *Bloomsbury Dictionary of Phrase & Allusion*. London: Bloomsbury.

Reisner, Robert (1971). *Graffiti: Two Thousand Years of Wall Writing*. Chicago: Henry Regnery Company.

Reynolds, Robert (1975). *Magic Symbols: A Photographic Study on Graffiti*. Portland, Oregon: Graphic Arts Center.

Ridout, Ronald and Clifford Witting (1969). *English Proverbs Explained*. London: Pan Books.

Röhrich, Lutz (1983). Anti-Sprichwörter: Zu einem neuen Buch von Wolfgang Mieder. *Muttersprache* 93, 351-354.

253

Rosten, Leo (1972). *Rome Wasn't Burned in a Day: The Mischief of Language*. Garden City, New York: Doubleday & Company.

Rowsome, Frank (1970). *Think Small. The Story of those Volkswagen Ads*. Brattleboro, Vermont: Stephen Greene Press.

Safian, Louis A. (1967). *The Book of Updated Proverbs*. New York: Abelard-Schuman.

Shaw, Susanna (1980). *Women in the John. A Collection of Graffiti from the Women's Room*. Berkeley, California: Creative Arts Book Company.

Simpson, John A. (1993). *The Concise Oxford Dictionary of Proverbs*. 3rd ed. Oxford: Oxford University Press.

Slung, Michele (1985). *Momilies "As My Mother Used to Say..."* New York: Ballantine Books.

Slung, Michele (1986). *More Momilies "As My Mother Used to Say..."* New York: Ballantine Books.

Stark, Judith (1982). *Priceless Proverbs...from the Tongue of the Young*. Los Angeles: Price, Stern, Sloan Publishers. (without pages).

Stewart, Susan A. *Nonsense: Aspects of Intertextuality in Folklore and Literature*. Baltimore, Maryland: Johns Hopkins University Press, 1978.

Still, James (1991). *The Wolfpen Notebooks: A Record of Appalachian Life*. Lexington, Kentucky: The University Press of Kentucky.

Thurber, James (1940). *Fables for Our Time and Famous Poems Illustrated*. New York, London: Harper & Brothers Publishers.

Thurber, James (1956). *Further Fables for Our Time*. New York: Simon and Schuster.

Tóthné Litovkina, Anna (1996). A Few Aspects of a Semiotic Approach to Proverbs, with Special Reference to Two Important American Publications [W. Mieder, *American Proverbs* (1989) and W. Mieder et al., *A Dictionary of American Proverbs* (1992)]. *Semiotica* 108, 307-380.

254

Walsh, W.S. (1892). *Handy-Book of Literary Curiosities*. Philadelphia: Lippincott.

Wanamaker, John (1908). *Wit and Humor of Business*. Philadelphia: George W. Jakobs Company.

Welch, Philip H. (1889). *Said is Fun*. New York: Charles Scribner's Sons.

Weller, Tom (1982). *Minims or, Man is the Only Animal that Wears Bow Ties*. Boston: Houghton Mifflin Co. (without pages).

Whiting, Barlett Jere (1989). *Modern Proverbs and Proverbial Sayings*. Cambridge, Massachusetts: Harvard University Press.

Whiting, Rudd (1910). *Four Hundred Good Stories*. New York: The Baker & Taylor Company.

Wilson, F.P. (1970). *The Oxford Dictionary of English Proverbs*. 3rd ed. Oxford: Oxford University Press (1st ed. 1935 by William George Smith).

Winick, Stephen D. (1998). *The Proverb Process: Intertextuality and Proverbial Innovation in Popular Culture*. Diss. University of Pennsylvania.

Woods, Barbara Allen (1968). Perverted Proverbs in Brecht and "Verfremdungssprache." *Germanic Review* 43, 100-108.

Woods, Ralph L. (1967). *The Modern Handbook of Humor*. New York: McGraw-Hill, Inc.

Wurdz, Gideon (1904). *The Foolish Dictionary*. Boston, Massachusetts: The Robinson, Luce Company. (without pages).

Yu, Timothy, and Jonathan Jang (1975). *The Thinking Man's Graffiti: Public Opinion from College and University Restrooms across the Nation*. Berkeley, California: Timco International.

Printed in the United States
26821LVS00002B/253-255

9 781875 943432